Genealogical
TROVES

~ VOLUME THREE

ALSO BY DENNIS FORD

Fiction

Red Star
Landsman
Things Don't Add Up
The Watchman
Tracks that Lead to Joy

Humor / Belles Lettres

Thinking About Everything
Miles of Thoughts
My Favorite Words
The Road Taken Again

Family History / Genealogy

Eight Generations
Genealogical Jaunts
Genealogical Musings
Genealogical Troves ~ Volume One
Genealogical Troves ~ Volume Two

Psychology

Lectures on Theories of Learning
Lectures on General Psychology ~ Volume One
Lectures on General Psychology ~ Volume Two

Genealogical
TROVES

~ VOLUME THREE

DENNIS FORD

GENEALOGICAL TROVES ~ VOLUME THREE

iUniverse books may be ordered through booksellers or by contacting:

iUniverse
1663 Liberty Drive
Bloomington, IN 47403
www.iuniverse.com
844-349-9409

ISBN: 978-1-6632-3730-9 (sc)
ISBN: 978-1-6632-3731-6 (e)

Print information available on the last page.

iUniverse rev. date: 03/22/2022

to the people of the past, that we remember them

I was going to add a subtitle—*Does Everyone in Ireland Have the Same First Name?*—but changed my mind out of respect for the people included in this volume. Probably, they used Irish names, family connections and sobriquets to distinguish among individuals. Lacking this information a century later, we're not so fortunate.

Contents

Preface

The quest to collect genealogical records pertaining to my ancestral septs has grown in scope since its inception. Originally conceived as two volumes, the number of records necessitated a third volume. This volume includes nineteenth century and early twentieth century records pertaining to—

- Hunt families residing in the vicinity of the market town of Ballyhaunis in County Mayo.

- Fitzmaurice families residing in the vicinity of Ballyhaunis.

Records for these families are limited to the civil and Roman Catholic Parishes of Annagh and Bekan in County Mayo and Kiltullagh Parish in County Roscommon. A few records document families in Aghamore and Knock parishes in County Mayo. Civil records for the parishes in County Mayo reside in the Claremorris registration district. Civil records for Kiltullagh parish reside in the Castlerea registration district of County Roscommon.

Civil records are available on-line at *www.irishgenealogy.ie*. Records for births and marriages commence in 1864. Death records commence in 1871. Records continue into the 1950s. They are searchable by name, year and registration district. (The latter facilitates searches, but is not required.) The website is periodically updated. In addition, the website contains select Roman Catholic church records. Unluckily, parishes in the vicinity of Ballyhaunis are not available.

Roman Catholic parish registers are available on-line at *www.registers. nli.ie*. The records terminate circa 1880. The records are searchable by event and date, not by surname. The legibility of the records, which are images of the parish registers, varies greatly. Records for Kiltullagh Parish are in excellent condition and legible. Early records for Bekan Parish are not always legible. The quality of the Annagh Parish records is deplorable. The handwriting of the priests is a scrawl from 1851 – 1870. In addition, the bottom sections of the on-line images are frequently blacked out and illegible. An additional, and nontrivial, problem with the Annagh and Bekan registers is that the pages are not always in chronological order. Depending on which priest entered the records, events in the same month and year could appear in different places in the register. (The chronological order improves in later registers.) As in the first two volumes, I elected to include only the month and year of individual records.

When I first became active in genealogy in the early 1990s I, like everyone else, used the microfilms created by the Church of Jesus Christ of Latter-Day Saints. Microfilms for both Annagh and Bekan parishes extended into the early twentieth century. It may be possible to consult *www.familysearch.org* in the event the microfilmed records were entered into the on-line database.

Census records for 1901 and 1911 are available at *www.census. nationalarchives.ie*. The records are searchable by surname and townland. Ballyhaunis records are searchable by street name.

Land records are available on-line at the Valuation Office at *www. irish-geneaography.com/valuation-office*. Griffith's Valuation is available at *www.askaboutireland.ie*. The Tithe Applotment Books are available at *www.titheapplotmentbooks.nationalarchives.ie*. The website of the National Archives of Ireland contains a number of interesting databases, including a Calendar of Wills that can be searched by surname, county and date of death. Find My Past (*www.findmypast.com*) has a huge selection of records including Ballyhaunis petty court records—an excellent trove of unique records. These records, which are not included in this volume, are available for a modest monthly fee.

All records in *Genealogical Troves ~ Volume Three* need to be verified. There may be errors in transcription—interpretation of handwriting is often analogous to interpreting a Rorschach card. Informants may have provided inaccurate details. Priests and civil registrars may have erred in recording events. Researchers who digitized the records may have made errors. Shamefully, I may have erred in copying names and dates.

Families had several months to report events to the authorities, so it can happen that the dates in the civil registers are discrepant from the dates of the actual events. (Families may have failed to report events to the civil authorities—this seems to have occurred most often with death records.) Unless there are corresponding baptism records, dates of births should be considered approximations. Dates of deaths and ages of decedents in civil records should also be considered approximations. Frequently, informants had only estimates of the decedents' actual ages.

Family records in *Genealogical Troves ~ Volume Three* should be considered incomplete—this is especially the case with older records. Baptisms and marriages that occurred before the commencement of church registers are permanently lost. Deaths and burials were not recorded by the churches included in this volume. Illegible handwriting may have resulted in overlooked records or in erroneous interpretations of names and dates. Prior to the 1870s, data from Annagh Parish are underrepresented in this volume. Pages may be missing from the extant church registers—chunks of pages appear to be missing in some registers.

Family records that appear in *Volume Three* are in chronological order from the first occurrence of names and events in parish registers or civil records. The names of godparents and witnesses in church records are in parentheses. Except for a few families, birth records in *Volume Three* generally terminate circa 1900. Marriage and death records continue to 1940. Parish names in marriage records are transcribed from the church registers. The parish of the bride was utilized for post-1864 marriages that have no matching church records. (This is an assumption.) The term "Bekan" refers to the parish name and not to the name of the townland, unless otherwise specified. Question marks are used to indicate uncertainties in transcribing names, dates and townlands. Where indicated, records require further verification.

Sources

Annagh Parish registers – Nov. 1851 – Nov. 1880

Bekan Parish registers – May 1832 – May 1872

Kiltullagh Parish registers – Augt. 1839 – Apr. 1881

Tuam Archdiocese Record of Marriages – 1821 – 1829

Civil Registers of Births, Claremorris & Castlerea districts – 1864 – circa 1900
Civil Registers of Marriages, Claremorris & Castlerea districts – 1864 – 1940
Civil Registers of Deaths, Claremorris & Castlerea districts – circa 1871 – 1940

Tithe Applotment Books – 1833

Griffith's Valuation – 1856

Calendar of Wills – 1858 - 1922

Hunt

The surname Hunt derives from O Fiachna, translated as "the hunt" or "the chase." The sept is part of the Siol Muireadaigh, descendants of King Muireadach Muillethan (died 702). In turn, the Siol Muireadaigh were part of the Ui Bruin Ai, descendants of Brion, half brother to Niall of the Nine Hostages. Brion lived in the late fourth/early fifth centuries. The Siol Muireadaigh inhabited Western Roscommon and included families of the MacDermotts and the O'Connors, kings of the region. The Hunt families were strongly localized in the vicinity of Ballyhaunis, especially in Annagh and Bekan Parishes.

An alternate origin of the Hunt sept is that it derives from the Ui Fiachrach, descendants of Fiachra, Brion's brother. This group of families was localized in Sligo, Mayo and Galway.

1796 Flax Seed Premium Entitlements

Hugh Hunt, Knock Parish

Diocese of Tuam Marriage Records

Patrick Hunt & Catherine Kilduff
m. June 1821 (John Hunt & Thomas Murphy), Aghamore & Knock Parish

Michael Hunt & Anne Swift
m. Sept. 1821 (Michael Morilly & Murdagh Finn), Bekan Parish

Hugh Hunt & Bridget Cunnane
m. Feb. 1822 (Malachy Hunt & Patrick Cunnane), Bekan

Mary Hunt & Patrick Bryan
m. Feb. 1822 (Patrick Fadrigal ? & James Sheridan), Bekan

Patrick Hunt & Mary Moran
m. Feb. 1822 (James Moran & Martin Grogan), Annagh Parish

Patrick Hunt & Bridget Kilroy
m. March 1822 (James Flanagan & Patrick Hufsey), Kiltullagh Parish

John Hunt & Mary Fitzgerald
m. Apr. 1822 (James Fitzgerald & James Hunt), Annagh

Hugh Hunt & Mary Kelly
m. Feb. 1823 (Michael Kelly & Hugh Kelly), Annagh

John Hunt & Anne Egan
m. Feb. 1823 (Philip Hunt & Patrick Hunt), Bekan

Mary Hunt & John Harkin
m. Apr. 1823 (Owen Harkin & Mary Hunt), Bekan

Bridget Hunt & John Smyth
m. Jan. 1824 (John Smyth & Bridget Caulfield), Bekan

John Hunt & Bridget Concannon
m. Feb. 1824 (Thomas Hunt & William Tarpey), Bekan

Patrick Hunt & Anne McNamara
m. March 1824 (John McNamara & John Murphy), Bekan

Michael Hunt & Mary Waldron
m. July 1825 (Michael Bourke & Richard Morrilly), Aghamore & Knock

Thomas Hunt & Margaret Lyons
m. Jan. 1826 (Patrick Lyons & Mary Lyons), Bekan

Bridget Hunt & Michael Hoster
m. Jan. 1826 (Simon Waldron & Margaret Hoster), Bekan

Bridget Hunt & John Muleheen,
m. Feb. 1826 (Thomas Mulken & Mary Jennings), Bekan

Bridget Hunt & Lacky Kelly
m. March 1826 (Edmond Kelly & John Brennan), Bekan

Catherine Hunt & Thomas Hidian (likely Kedian)
m. Nov. 1826 (John Hunt & William Kedian), Annagh

James Hunt & Margaret Hidian (likely Kedian)
m. July 1827 (Patrick Drudy & Michael Hidian), Annagh

Tithe Applotment Books, 1833

John Hunt - Lecarrow, Annagh Parish

John Hunt - Redhill, Annagh

Thomas Hunt - Island, Bekan Parish

John Hunt - Larganboy East & West, Bekan

John Hunt - Spaddagh, Bekan

Walter Hunt – Cloonaheace, Knock Parish

Griffith's Valuation – 1856

Catherine Hunt – Lecarrow, Annagh Parish

Dennis Ford

James Hunt – Lecarrow

James Hunt – Derrynacong

James Hunt – Scregg

John Hunt – Lecarrow

Malachy Hunt – Knockanarra

Mary Hunt – Derrynacong

Murtagh Hunt – Lecarrow

Patrick Hunt – Lecarrow

Philip Hunt – Moneymore

Thomas Hunt – Derrynacong

Thomas Hunt – Killunaugher

Thomas Hunt – Lecarrow

Thomas Hunt – Leo

Anthony Hunt – Belesker, Bekan Parish

Hugh Hunt – Derrymore

James Hunt – Bekan

James Hunt – Brackloon South

John Hunt – Bekan

John Hunt – Cloonbookoughter

Mark Hunt – Bohogerawer

Mark Hunt – Bracklaghboy

Mary Hunt – Bohogerawer

Patrick Hunt – Island

Patrick Hunt (John) – Larganboy East

Patrick Hunt (Lacky) – Larganboy East

Patrick Hunt – Skeaghard

Thomas Hunt – Bohogerawer

Thomas Hunt – Bracklaghboy

Thomas Hunt – Cuiltycreaghan

Thomas Hunt – Reask

William Hunt – Bohogerawer

William Hunt – Bracklaghboy

William Hunt – Cloonbookoughter

Bridget Hunt – Cloonfad East, Kiltullagh Parish

Michael Hunt – Gorteen

Patrick Hunt – Pollanalty East

James Hunt – Cloondace, Knock Parish

James Hunt – Derradda

Patrick Hunt – Cloonlee

William Hunt – Crockaunrannell

Honoria Hunt – Liscosker, Aghamore Parish

John Hunt – Balloor

John Hunt – Cloontarriff

John Hunt – Falleighter

Michael Hunt – Falleighter

Thomas Hunt – Balloor

Thomas Hunt – Cloontarriff

Thomas Hunt – Cloonturk

William Hunt – Balloor

William Hunt – Cloontarriff

William Hunt – Mannin

Annagh, Bekan & Kiltullagh Parish Registers, Baptisms and Marriages

Thomas Hunt & Mary Lyons
Child, May 1832 (sponsors illegible), Bekan

John Hunt & Catherine ?
Bridget, July 1832 (Patrick ? & Mary Hunt), Bekan

Margaret Hunt ? & ?? (record requires verification]
Kitty ?, July 1832 (Darby Groarke & Bridget Cox), Bekan

? Hunt & Michael Ward
Catherine, Augt. 1832 (Austin Waldron & Honora Cribbin), Bekan

Honor Hunt & Brian Lofnan
Thomas, Augt. 1832 (Brian Lofnan & Mary Hunt), Bekan

Note: this may be the same couple listed below as ? Hunt & Bartholomew Lohan. And see the reference below to Honor Hunt & Bernard Loghan.

Bridget Hunt & John Mul-
Bridget, Oct. 1832 (John Moran & Bridget ?), Bekan

Note: see the reference to Bridget Hunt & John Muleheen in the Tuam Marriage Records.

Thomas Hunt & Margaret Farr / Fair ? [name requires verification]
Mary, Nov. 1832 (Michael Hunt), Bekan
Child, Dec. 1837 (John Hunt & Mary Hunt), Bekan [record requires verification]
Patrick, March 1845 (Patrick Hunt & Bridget Hunt)

Catherine Hunt & B-
Child, Dec. 1833 (Thomas Hunt & ? Doyle), Bekan

Patrick Hunt & Mary Hunt
m. Jan. 1834 (James Hunt & Margaret Kelly), Bekan

Patrick Hunt & ? Mullowney
m. Feb. 1834 (Patrick Fitzmaurice & Kitty Harly ?), Bekan

? Hunt & Bartholomew Lohan
Cicely, Feb. 1834 (Michael Lohan & Hugh Hunt), Bekan

Elizabeth Hunt & Patrick Dyer
m. March 1834 (Timothy Cuddy & Peggy Hunt), Bekan [date requires verification]
Martin, Nov. 1844 (Thomas Hunt & Mary Dyer), Bekan

Bridget Hunt & Mark Fitzmaurice
Thomas, Sept. 1834 (Philip Hunt & Mary Hunt), Bekan
John, 1836 (? Carroll & Mary Anne Carroll) [date requires verification]
Mary Oct. 1837 (Patrick Fitzmaurice & Catherine Sloyan)
John, Apr. 1846 (Edward Hunt & Sara Hunt)

Bridget Hunt & Edmond Comer
Thomas, Jan. 1835 (Lackey Hunt & K- Hunt), Bekan
Edmund, Dec. 1846 (Thomas M- & Mary M-)

Bridget Hunt & Patrick Swift
Patrick, Jan. 1835 (John Hunt & Bridget O'Gara), Bekan

Mary Hunt & Luke Higgins
m. Feb. 1835 (Pat Carney & Mary ?), Bekan

Note: see record below for Bridget Hunt & Luke Higgins.

? Hunt & Thomas Fitzmaurice
Hannah ?, June 1835 (sponsors illegible), Bekan [record requires verification]

Thomas Hunt & Bridget Tighe
Sally, July 1835 (John Finn & Catherine Hunt), Bekan
John, Nov. 1836 (Patrick Hunt & Judy Tighe)
Patrick, Sept. 1838 (Michael Hunt & Mary Hunt)

Thomas Hunt & Peggy Lyons
Thomas, Augt. 1835 (Henry Fitzmaurice & ? Grogan), Bekan

Note: see the reference to Thomas Hunt & Margaret Lyons in the Tuam
Marriage Records.

Patrick Hunt & Penelope Jennings
m. Nov. 1835 (Martin Hunt & Bridget Hunt), Bekan
Catherine, Augt. 1836 (James Hunt & Nelly Jennings)
Mary, Dec. 1838 (Patrick Boyle & Mary Fahey), Island
Patrick, Dec. 1844 (Thomas Hunt & Mary Lyons) [date requires verification]

Patrick Hunt & Anne Hunt
Mary ?, 1835 (Thomas Hunt & Bridget Hunt), Bekan [record requires verification]

Honor Hunt & Bernard Loghan
Bridget, May 1836 (Patrick Morrilly & Honor Hunt), Bekan

Patrick Hunt & Betty Neiland
Mary, July 1836 (Patrick O'Hara & Catherine Hunt), Bekan

Catherine Hunt & Patrick O'Hara
m. July 1836 (Owen Lowry & Mary Hunt), Bekan
James, Augt. 1845 (Mary ?), Bekan

Mary Hunt & James Kearns
Catherine, July 1836 (Bryan Kearns & Bridget Kearns), Bekan

Margaret Hunt & Patrick Waldron
Augustine, Nov. 1836 (John Hunt & ? Hunt), Bekan
Bridget, Augt. 1838 (? Holian ? & Mary Hunt)

Hugh Hunt & Mary Lyons
Patrick, 1836 (John Hunt & Mary Boyle), Bekan [date requires verification]

Patrick Hunt & Betty Hunt
Honor, 1836 (sponsors illegible), Bekan [record requires verification]

John Hunt & Bridget Hunt
Child, 1836 (?? & Bridget McGuire), Bekan [date requires verification]

Thomas Hunt & Catherine Moran
Bridget, Feb. 1837 (James Hunt & Margaret Hunt), Bekan

Thomas Hunt & Bridget Farrell
m. May 1837 (Brian Loghan & Mary Farrell), Bekan
Peter, May 1838 (Brian Loghan & Bridget Curley)
Margaret, Dec. 1845 (A. Smyth & Mary Farrell)

Mary Hunt & Murty Johnson
Margaret, Sept. 1837 (James Jordan & Mary Johnson), Bekan

Michael Hunt & Anne Swift
Michael, Oct. 1837 (Philip Swift & Bridget Tarpey), Bekan

Note: see the reference to Michael Hunt & Anne Swift in the Tuam Marriage Records.

Ann Hunt & Patrick Hopkins
Michael, Dec. 1837 (John Hunt & Mary Grogan ?), Bekan
Patrick, Apr. 1843 (John McGreal & Ellen Hunt)

Note: in Patrick's record the mother's name was given as Catherine.

Mary Hunt & Bernard Coll [name requires verification]
m. March 1838 (Patrick Egan & Bridget Grogan), Bekan

Patrick Hunt & Mary Neiland
m. May 1838 (James Hunt & Bridget Neiland), Bekan
Mary, Jan. 1845 (Thomas Mullaney & Mary Hunt), Bekan
James, Augt. 1846 (James Hunt & Ellen Greally)

Bridget Hunt & John Finn [name requires verification]
Mary ?, Sept. 1838 (C- & Catherine Finn)

John Hunt & Mary ?
Catherine, Oct. 1838 (Michael Hunt & Catherine Cribbin), Bekan

John Hunt & ? Tarpey
Nelly, Oct. 1838 (James Cribbin & Mary L-), Bekan

Nelly Hunt & Edward Gibbons
Edward, Nov. 1839 (Michael Connelly & C-), Cloonfad, Kiltullagh

Bridget Hunt & Patrick Kilroy
Mary, Feb. 1840 (James Kilroy & Mary Grogan) Ballybane Upper, Kiltullagh
Margaret, Sept. 1842 (John Crosby & Mary Hunt)

Mary Hunt & Patrick Plunkett
m. March 1840 (John Hunt & Mary Murphy), Bekan

Hu Hunt ? & Nancy Glynn
Michael, 1840 (Michael Glynn & Mary Tighe), Bekan

John Hunt & Bridget Ronan
David, Jan. 1841 (Michael Hunt & Winifred Connor), Kiltobar, Kiltullagh
Anne, Augt. 1842 (Thomas Regan & ? Gibbons)
William, Feb. 1845 (?? & ? Rooney)

Michael Hunt & Ellen Regan
Certificate issued to Michael Hunt to marry outside parish, Feb. 1841
Michael, Sept. 1843 (Mary Waldron), Gorteen, Kiltullagh
Mary, July 1845 (Barbara Waldron)
Mary, March 1846 (Honor P -)
Thomas, Dec. 1847 (Mary Fahy)

Patrick Hunt & Bridget Hett
m. Jan. 1842 (Michael Hett & Sara Hett), Kiltobar
Thomas, Dec. 1842 (Catherine Hett)
Mary, March 1846 ? (Nelly Malley)
David, July 1857 (David Hunt & Margaret Nally ?)
Bridget, July 1859 (? Hett & Anne Connally)
Anne, November, 1866 (John ? & James Kedian), Pollanalty

Patrick Hunt & Catherine Owens
Mary, March 1843 (Thomas Hunt & Bridget Hinnegan ?), Bekan
Thomas, Dec. 1852 (Thomas Owens & Judith Owens)
James, Apr. 1855 (James McHale & Bridget McHale)

James Hunt & Bridget Grealy
Thomas, June 1843 (Michael Hopkins & Bridget Hopkins), [date requires verification]
James, Augt. 1845 (James Hunt & Penelope Jennings), Bekan

James Hunt & Mary McHale
Martin, Nov. 1844 (Martin ? & Bridget Hunt), Bekan
Mary, Feb. 1852 (Martin Kelly & Mary Waldron)

James Hunt & Honor Fitzmaurice
m. Jan. 1845 (Michael Hunt & Honor Flatley), Bekan
Ellen, Nov. 1854 (Thomas Fitzmaurice & Biddy Morley), Annagh
Child, Oct. 1858 (Mary Waldron & John Fitzmaurice)
Child, ?? 1862 (? & Thomas Fitzmaurice) [record requires verification]

Mark Hunt & Catherine Lyons
John, Apr. 1845 (Hugh Lyons & Margaret Comber), Bekan

Catherine Hunt & Thad Hopkins
James, Augt. 1845 (James Hunt & Bridget Hunt)
Margaret, Jan. 1854 (James T- & Bridget Hopkins), Larganboy
Michael, March 1857 (James Hopkins & Bridget Lyons)

Thomas Hunt & Nancy Flynn
Lackey, Sept. 1845 (Michael Flynn & Mary ?), Bekan

Ellen Hunt & Thady Donlan
m. Nov. 1845 (Thomas Gormally & Mary Hunt), Bekan

Patrick Hunt & Catherine ? [name requires verification]
Catherine, Nov. 1845 (Thomas Hunt & Judith ?), Bekan

Bridget Hunt & Thomas Cunnane
m. March 1846 (James Caulfield & Bridget Fahy), Bekan

Brian Hunt & Mary Tighe
Thomas, Sept. 1846 (Patrick O'Brien & Mary Cribbin), Bekan

James Hunt & Sarah Cunnane
John, Jan. 1847 (James Moran & Bridget Hunt), Bekan
Mary, July 1848 (Patrick Cunnane & Kitty Cunnane)
Child, Feb. 1851 (Michael Hunt & ? Hunt) [record requires verification]
Patrick, March 1856 (Thomas Cunnane & Bridget Hunt)
Ellen, Jan. 1858 (Patrick Kelly & Margaret O'Dowd)
Margaret, Jan. 1862 (Patrick Hunt & Mary Hunt)

Bridget Hunt & Thomas Runnane [name requires verification]
Mary, Feb. 1847 (James Kerins & ??), Bekan

? Hunt & Mary Flatley [name requires verification]
Ellen, March 1847 (Martin Darcy & Bridget ?), Bekan

Thomas Hunt & Mary Finan [name requires verification]
Thomas, June 1847 (Patrick Nary & Mary Grogan), Bekan

Patrick Hunt & Catherine Morris
Patrick, June 1848 (Michael Owens & Bridget Hunt), Bekan

Bridget Hunt & Martin Fitzmaurice
Patrick, June 1848 (John Keadon & Mary Keadon), Bekan

Patrick Hunt & Catherine Quinn [name requires verification]
Catherine, Augt. 1848 (Patrick Hunt & Mary Lyden)

Mary Hunt & Martin ?
m. Jan. 1849 (Patrick Fitzmaurice & ??), Bekan

Mary Hunt & James Barnicle
John, May 1849 (John Hughes & Mary Murphy), Bekan
Mary, May 1854 (Thomas Rattican & Mary Conway)

Thomas Hunt & Bridget Cunnane
Thomas, May 1849 (Mark Hunt & Honor Finnegan), Bekan [record requires verification]

Honor Hunt & Brian Soylan [name requires verification—likely Sloyan]
Ellen, Dec. 1849 (? & Catherine Kilfoyle), Bekan

Mark Hunt & Honora Tigue
Bridget, Jan. 1850 (Thomas Hunt & Margaret Hunt), Bekan

Note: this couple may be the same as Mark Hunt & Honoria Finn (see below).

Patrick Hunt & Elizabeth ? [name requires verification]
Bridget, Augt. 1850 (John Hunt & Margaret Hunt), Bekan

Patrick Hunt & Margaret Gunnigan
Mary, Nov. 1850 (Patrick Navin ? & Bridget Jennings), Bekan
Patrick, Nov. 1852 (Thomas Spelman & Bridget McKeown)

Mary Hunt & John Groarke
Catherine, Nov. 1850 (John Hunt & Mary Mulkeen), Bekan
James, Augt. 1857 (Bridget Frehily)
Bridget, March 1860 (no sponsors listed)

Thomas Hunt & Catherine Burns
Bridget, 1851 [record requires verification], Leo
Margaret, 1853 [record requires verification]
Anne, 1859 [record requires verification]

John Hunt & Mary Hunt
Julianna, Jan. 1851 (Patrick Hunt & Bridget Hunt), Bekan
Austin, July 1858 (Darby Hunt & Bridget Hunt)

Thomas Hunt & ? Hunt [name requires verification]
Child, Feb. 1851 (James Brennan & Mary Caulfield), Bekan

John Hunt & Bridget Hunt
John, May 1851 (Patrick Tarpey & Mary Carrol ?), Cloonfad
James, July 1855 (Martin Brennan & Bridget Walsh), Killunaugher
Catherine, May 1856 (Murty Hunt & Bridget Hunt)
Mary, 1857 (sponsors illegible) [record requires verification]
John, Oct. 1861 (Mark Hunt & Mary Duffy)

Mark Hunt & Honoria Finn
Martin, Oct. 1851 (Patrick Waldron & Catherine Killian), Bekan
Michael, Sept. 1856 (Patrick Judge & Bridget Waldron)
Thomas, June 1859 (Martin Hunt & Bridget Freeman)
Philip, May 1861 (Thomas Hunt & Margaret Hunt)
Honoria, March 1864 (Richard Henry & Bridget Hunt) [record requires verification]
Mary, Augt. 1867 (Martin Hunt & Bridget Waldron), Bracklaghboy
Catherine, Apr. 1871 (Mark Hunt & Mary Hunt)

Note: in Honoria's record the father's name was given as Patrick.

Patrick Hunt & Bridget Hunt
Catherine, March 1852 (Patrick ? & Anne Ruane), Gorteen, Kiltullagh

Mary Hunt & Peter Flynn
m. Nov. 1852 (Patrick Kelly & Mary Hunt)
Anne, 1853 (Mary Hunt), Clooncrim, Kiltullagh
Bridget, Feb. 1855 (James Gannon & Mary Hunt)

Note: Mary was from Derrynacong.

Bridget Hunt & John ?
John, 1852 (Bridget ?), Annagh [record requires verification]

Patrick Hunt & Bridget Fitzmaurice
m. Feb. 1853 (Peter Fitzmaurice & Bridget Loftus), Kiltullagh
Mary, Augt. 1854 (Patrick Flynn & Bridget Hunt), Laughil
Hugh, Jan. 1858 (James Cox & Anne Dodd)
Patrick, Nov. 1859 (Patrick Fitzmaurice & Bridget Fitzmaurice)
Michael, Oct. 1862 (Catherine Discon)
Thomas, Jan. 1870 (Timothy Flynn & Catherine Flynn)

Note: Patrick was from Annagh Parish. Bridget was from Laughil.

Thomas Hunt & Bridget Brennan
m. March 1853 (John Forde & Bridget Hunt), Kelane ?, Annagh
Child, 1857 (Hugh Hunt & N- Hunt) [record needs to be verified]

James Hunt & Mary Hunt
Thomas, Apr. 1853 (Margaret Tarpey & Mary Hunt), Bekan

Francis ? Hunt & Mary Hunt [name requires verification]
John, June 1853 (James Meehan & Sarah Devany), Bekan

Bridget Hunt & Michael Fahy
m. Jan. 1854 (John Fahy & Catherine Flynn), Bekan

Ellen Hunt & Patrick Donnellan
m. Feb. 1854 (William Beasty & Honor Hunt), Bekan

Bridget Hunt & Martin Duggan
m. Feb. 1854 (William Kirrane and Ann Grogan), Bekan
Bridget, Dec. 1854 (Michael Walsh & Mary Duggan)
Thomas, Oct. 1856 (John Hunt & Mary Duggan)
Mary, June 1859 (Thomas Hunt & Anne Mulloy)
Mary, July 1861 (James Duggan & Catherine Glavey)
Anne, Dec. 1862 (James Duggan & Mary Cunnane)

Bridget Hunt & James Cox
m. Dec. 1854 (Hugh Cox & Bridget Fitzmaurice), Annagh
Thomas, Nov. 1855 (Patrick Hunt & Mary Cox), Derrynacong
Child, Feb. 1858 (Hugh Cox & Bridget Fitzmaurice),
Child, 1860 (no sponsors listed)
Margaret, Dec. 1864 (civil record)
Bridget, Augt. 1867 (civil record; Mary Hunt of Bargariff present)
Kate, May 1871 (John Cox & Bridget Hunt; Catherine Kelly of Derrynacong present)

Patrick Hunt & Mary Hunt
Patrick, 1854 (Murty Hunt & Mary Hopkins), Annagh Parish

Hugh Hunt & Margaret Brennan
m. Feb. 1855 (Brian Loughin & Mary Cuddy), Annagh
James, Nov. 1864 (civil record, Bridget Brennan, aunt), Leo

John Hunt & Bridget Waldron
m. March 1855 (John Judge & Mary Waldron), Bekan Parish
Michael, ? 1861 (James Walron & Ellen Waldron) [date requires verification]
Ellen, March 1865 (civil record), Lecarrow
James, Jan. 1867 (civil record)
Mary, July 1869 (John Murphy & Bridget Hunt)
John, July 1871 (Michael Waldron & Kate Hunt)
Anne, Dec. 1873 (Michael Waldron & Bridget Caulfield)
Honoria, Sept. 1876 (John Murphy & Kate Hunt)
Austin, Augt. 1878 (civil record)
Thomas, Nov. 1880 (civil record0

Mary Hunt & Patrick Meath
m. May 1855 (James Lyons & Bridget Hunt), Bekan
Catherine, Augt. 1857 (James Meath & Honor Flanagan)
Denis, Apr. 1856 (John Hunt & Mary Meath)
Honor, May 1859 (Michael Meath & Catherine Finnegan)

Note: see record below for Mary Hunt & Patrick Meehan.

Thomas Hunt & Nelly ? Hunt [name requires verification]
Anne, Oct. 1855 (John Hunt & Ann Hunt), Annagh

James Hunt & Mary Frehily
m. Dec. 1855 (Austin Frehily & Bridget Frehily), Bekan
Ellen, Feb. 1860 (James Frehily & Honoria Holsten ?), Bekan
Thomas, Apr. 1862 (Martin ? & Catherine Frehily)

Note: this maybe the same couple listed below as James Hunt & Mary Freely.

Catherine Hunt & Michael K-
m. Jan. 1856 (James Hunt & Mary A. Hunt), Annagh

Bridget Hunt & Luke Higgins
Catherine, Feb. 1856 (Thomas Higgins & Mary K-), Bekan

Bridget, Dec. 1858 (James Kearns & Mary Kearns)
Bridget, Oct. 1861 (Michael Higgins & Mary Cunnane)

Note: mother's name was given as Mary in the second Bridget record.

William Hunt & Bridget Hunt
Anne, Nov. 1856 (William Keegan & Bridget Hunt), Bekan
Catherine, Jan. 1858 (Patrick Hunt & Mary Hunt)
Mary, June 1859 (Thomas Hunt & Elizabeth Hunt) [record requires verification]
Catherine, Sept. 1864 (civil record), Cloonbook
Philip, Oct.1866 (civil record; Mary Freely of Gorteen present)
Elizabeth, Nov. 1868 (civil record)
Ellen, Feb. 1871 (civil record; Mary Freely of Derrymore present)
Margaret, Oct. 1872 (civil record)
William, Oct. 1874 (civil record)
Bridget, March 1877 (civil record)
Honoria, Oct. 1880 (civil record)

Note: in Mary's record the mother's maiden name was given as Dempsey.

Murtagh Hunt & Bridget Hunt
m. 1856 (Thomas Freely & Mary Waldron) [date requires verification]
Child ? 1857 (William Hunt & Nelly ? Hunt), Annagh
John, Feb. ? 1861 (John Hunt & Ellen Hunt)
Catherine, Augt. 1862 (John Hunt & Celia Hunt) [date requires verification]
James, Jan. 1866 (civil record), Lecarrow
Mary, Augt. 1868 (civil record)
Ellen, Feb. 1871 (John Hunt & Kate Hunt)
Austin, June 1873 (Michael Cribbin & Bridget Freely ?; Mary Groarke present)
Bridget, Sept. 1877 (John Hunt & Anne Hunt)
Child, Sept. 1879 (civil record)

Michael Hunt & Bridget Hunt
m. Feb. 1857 (Thomas Freely & Mary Waldron), Bekan

Lackey Hunt & Mary Hunt
Austin, ? 1857 (Patrick Hunt & Berf. Car-), Annagh [date requires verification]
Patrick, May 1860 (Patrick Waldron & Bridget F-)

Note: see the reference below to Lackey Hunt & Margaret Carney.

Mary Hunt & Patrick Meehan
Honoria, May 1858 (Michael Meehan & Catherine Finnegan)
Patrick, March 1864 (Michael Prendergast & Bridget Morley), Cloonlara, Bekan

Catherine Hunt & ? Golden
William, 1858 (William Hunt & Anne Rodgers), Annagh [date requires verification]
Judith, ? 1860 (Patrick B- & Judy Morrell) [record requires verification]

Mary Hunt & Thomas Kelly
m. Jan. 1859 (J. Kelly & Mary Drudy), Annagh
William, Oct. 1859 (? & Mary Kelly)
Catherine, Oct. 1860 (Michael Raftery & Mary ?)
Bridget, Augt. 1864, (civil record), Killunaugher)
Mary, Dec. 1866 (civil record)
Michael, Nov. 1868 (Thomas Freely & Catherine Freely; Anne Kelly present)

Note: Mary Hunt was the daughter of Thomas Hunt of Derrynacong.

Luke Hunt & Peggy Hunt
Mary, March 1859 (D. Hunt & Mary Duffy), Annagh Parish

Anne Hunt & Peter Fleming
m. Apr. 1859 (Martin Mannion & Mary Hunt), Kiltullagh
James, Sept. 1860 (John Ronan & Catherine Rogers), Cloonfad
Bridget, Feb. 1866 (Thomas Fleming & Bridget R-)
John, Sept. 1867 (James ? & Ellen Ronan)
Catherine, Jan. 1871 (Jane Fleming & Anne Hunt; Mary Kedian of Pollanalty present)

Luke, Sept. 1872 (Anthony Mullin & Mary Fleming)
Anne, Jan. 1876 (Stephen & Catherine R-)
Winifred, July 1877 (Patrick Ronayne & Winny Rogers)

Mary Hunt & Cormac Rogers
Winifred, Nov. 1859 (Peter Prendergast & Eleanor Prendergast), Kiltullagh
Peter, May, 1861 (Thomas Rogers & Catherine Quinn), Cloonfad

Mary Hunt & Thomas Forde
m. Feb. 1860 (Thomas Kelly ? & Mary Hunt) Annagh
Catherine, Dec. 1861 (Patrick Hunt & Catherine Hunt), Reask
Patrick, Augt. 1864 (Hugh Forde & Catherine Hunt)
Anne, Dec. 1869 (Thomas Hunt ? & Ellen Mulhern), Larganboy
Mary, Jan. 1873 (civil record)

John Hunt & Anne Grogan
John, June 1860 (Patrick McGreal & Margaret Hunt)
William, June 1862 (Matthew Hunt & Honoria Hunt)
Thomas, Apr. 1865 (Thomas Grogan & Mary Grogan), Bracklaghboy
Mary, Feb. 1868 (James Grogan & Befida ? Grogan)
Honoria, Feb. 1870 (Michael Walsh & Honoria ?)
Bridget, Sept. 1871 (civil record)
Catherine, Augt. 1873 (civil record; Mary McGrath of Greenwood present)

Note: father's name was given as Patrick in Mary's record.

Judith Hunt & Patrick Morley
Michael, June 1860 (John Morley & Mary Morley), Bekan

Mary Hunt & Bernard Kyne (Coyne)
m. Feb. 1861 (John McDonnell & Mary Hunt), Bekan

Note: see record below of Mary Hunt & Bryan Kyne.

Bridget Hunt & James Mulloy
m. Feb. 1861 (John Hunt), Annagh [date requires verification]

Catherine Hunt & Patrick Swift
m. March 1861 (John Swift & Mary Hunt), Bekan
Patrick, Jan. 1864 (Thomas Hunt & Mary Hunt), Ballyhaunis
Andrew, Feb. 1866 (Patrick Hunt & Mary Hunt)
Bridget, Sept. 1868 (Patrick Hunt & Margaret Hunt)

Honoria Hunt & William Forde
m. March 1861 (Michael Waldron & Kitty Grogan), Bekan
Margaret, Oct. 1863 (John Hunt & Mary Ford), Reask
Michael, Nov. 1865 (Thomas Forde & Catherine Forde)
Bridget, Oct. 1867 (Thomas Forde & Bridget Duggan)
Patrick, 1870 (Patrick Forde & Catherine Moran)
John, July 1875 (Patrick Forde & Mary Forde)

Mary Hunt & Walter Waldron
m. Apr. 1861 (Patrick Waldron & Catherine Hunt), Bekan
John, 1866 (James Fahy & Bridget Waldron), Derrymore

John Hunt & Julia McGuire
Ellen, Oct. 1861 (John McGuire & Ellen McGuire), Bekan

Thomas Hunt & Mary Hunt
Catherine, Dec. 1861 (Patrick Hunt & Catherine Hunt), Bekan

Mary Hunt & John Mulkeen
m. Feb. 1862 (Martin Mannion & Mary Hunt), Bekan

Thomas Hunt & Mary Fitzmaurice
m. Feb. 1863 (John Hunt & Mary Flatley), Bekan
William, Nov. 1864 (Patrick Fitzmaurice & Margaret Fitzmaurice), Brackloon
Thomas, July 1867 (civil record; Catherine Fitzmaurice present), Lisbaun

Bridget Hunt & Thomas Caulfield
m. March 1863 (John Higgins & Margaret Darcy), Bekan
John, Jan. 1864 (Bernard Caulfield & Ellen Hunt), [record requires verification]

Mary Hunt & Bryan Kyne
Bridget, July 1863 (Catherine Hunt), Clooncrim

Margaret Hunt & Patrick Brennan
m. Jan. 1864 (Michael Keane & Cecilia Lyons)
Edward, Dec. 1864 (John Hunt & Catherine Keane), Scregg
Martin, Sept. 1868 (Patrick Hunt & Ellen Brennan)
Patrick, Sept. 1870 (James Hunt & ? Hunt)

Note: Mary was the daughter of Patrick Hunt of Clagnagh. Patrick was
the son of Martin Brennan of Kiltobar.

Anne Hunt & Stephen Ronayne / Ronan
m. Jan. 1864 (Patrick Ronayne & Mary Barret), Kiltullagh
Patrick, Jan. 1865 (Patrick Ronan & Bridget Ronan), Cloonfad
James, Dec. 1866 (Michael Ronayne & Catherine Gildea ?)
Bridget, Nov. 1871 (Thomas Ronan & Mary Waldron)
Bridget, Dec. 1872 (John Hunt & Mary Hunt)
Anne Mary, Nov. 1875 (? Kilday ? & Winny Rogers)

Note: Anne was the daughter of Thomas Hunt of Cloonfad. Stephen was
the son of Thomas Ronayne of Ballykilleen. The civil record listed Anne
Mary as Hanna Mary.

Thomas Hunt & Mary Nowlan
m. Apr. 1864 (Darby Hunt & Catherine Nolan), Bekan

Note: no civil record has been located for this marriage.

William Hunt & Honoria Healy
m. May 1864 (Pat Killeen & Catherine Murphy), Bekan

Note: William was the son of Thomas Hunt of Killknock. Honoria was
the daughter of John Healy of Killknock.

James Hunt & Mary Freely
Honoria, June 1864 (James McGarry & Bridget Hunt), Scregg

Anne, July 1866 (civil record)
James, Oct. 1868 (civil record)
Martin, Dec. 1870 (John Hunt & Catherine Hunt)
Elizabeth, Apr. 1873 (civil record)
Patrick, Sept. 1875 (civil record; Ellen Hunt of Scregg present)

Patrick Hunt & Bridget Murtagh
James, July 1864, Cloonlee, Kiltullagh [record requires verification]

John Hunt & Catherine Moran
Patrick, Dec. 1864 (Patrick Fitzmaurice & Honoria Hunt)
Thomas, March 1866 (civil record), Reask
Margaret, Augt. 1867 (civil record; Thomas Hunt, father-in-law, present)
Bridget, Nov. 1869 (civil record)
Anne, Augt. 1875 (civil record; Margaret Doogan of Reask present)

Michael Hunt & Mary Mulkeen
m. March 1865 (Bryan Grealy & Bridget Nolan), Bekan
Bridget, Jan. 1867 (civil record), Bekan townland
John, May 1870 (civil record)
Mary, Nov. 1872 (civil record)
Michael, May 1874 (civil record)
Thomas, Augt. 1876 (civil record; Margaret Hunt of Bekan present)

Note: Michael was the son of John Hunt of Bekan. Mary was the daughter of Thomas Mulkeen of Larganboy.

Mary Hunt & Michael Fynn
m. Feb. 1866 (Thomas Morris & Honor Lowry), Bekan

Note: Mary was the daughter of Bryan Hunt of Cloonacurry, Bekan. Michael was the son of Patrick Fynn of Killunaugher.

Honoria Hunt & Michael Flatley
m. April 1866 (William Moran & Mary Fitzmaurice), Bekan
Catherine, Dec. 1867 (William Flatley & Bridget Hunt), Corrasluastia, Kiltullagh

Catherine, June 1869 (civil record; Mary Moran of Corrasluastia present)
Bridget, Dec. 1870 (James Flatley & Anne Hunt), Ganiveen [requires verification]
Mary, Nov. 1873 (William Flatley & Catherine Freeley)
Anne, Augt. 1874 (William Flatley & Mary Flatley)
Mary, Augt. 1879 (William Flatley & Bridget Moran), Corraluastia

Note: Honoria was the daughter of Philip Hunt of Moneymore. Michael was the son of Martin Flatley of Ganiveen, Kiltullagh.

John Hunt & Honoria Tarpey
m. Apr. 1866 (Patrick Higgins & Mary Murphy) Aghamore Parish
Ellen, Apr. 1871 (civil record; Mary Brennan of Kiltobar present), Clagnagh
Patrick, Feb. 1873 (civil record; Catherine Lyons of Clagnagh present)
John Austin, June 1875 (civil record; Anne Morley of Clagnagh prrsent)
Mary, Oct. 1877 (civil record)
Honoria, Sept. 1880 (civil record; Mary Higgins of Knockbrack present)
Bridget, Jan. 1883 (civil record; Catherine Lyons present)
James, Jan. 1885 (civil record)
Catherine, Nov. 1887 (civil record; Ellen Hunt present)

John was the son of Patrick Hunt of Clagnagh. Honoria, age 19, was the daughter of Dominick Tarpey of Mannin, Aghamore Parish

Lackey Hunt & Margaret Carney
Margaret, Augt. 1866 (civil record), Knockanarra, Annagh

Patrick Hunt & Anne Hunt
m. Feb. 1867 (Augustine Hunt & Margaret Hunt), Annagh
Mary, Feb. 1868 (civil record), Lecarrow
Bridget, July 1869 (Murty Hunt & Honora Hunt)
Catherine, Oct. 1870 (Thomas Hunt & Bridget Costello)
Patrick, Sept. 1872 (John Hunt & Bridget Hunt)
Ellen, Nov. 1875 (Murty Hunt & Bridget Hunt)
Honoria, Oct. 1877 (civil record)
Anne, July 1879 (civil record) [note - date verified in civil records]
Anne, Nov. 1879 (civil record)

James, Dec. 1880 (civil record; Mary Hunt of Lecarrow present)
Mary, Oct. 1882 (civil record; Bridget Hunt of Lecarrow present)
Anne, March 1884 (civil record)
Maggie, Jan. 1886 (civil record)
John Thomas, Oct. 1887 (civil record; Kate Hunt present)

Note: Patrick was the son of Patrick Hunt, dec'd., of Lecarrow. Anne was the daughter of James Hunt of Derryfad.

Mary Hunt & Edmond Moran
m. March 1867 (Martin Moran & Margaret Hunt), Bekan

Note: Mary was the daughter of Patrick Hunt of Island. Edmond was the son of Bartholomew Moran, dec'd., of Carrickmacantire, Annagh.

Margaret Hunt & Patrick Moran
m. Augt. 1867 (John Moran & Catherine Hunt), Annagh

Note: Margaret, age 24, was the daughter of Thomas Hunt of Coolnafarna. Patrick, age 26, was the son of Thomas Moran, dec'd., of Derrymore.

Margaret Hunt & Martin Carney
m. Jan. 1868 (Richard Murphy & Mary Murphy), Bekan
Austin, Dec. 1969 (Anthony Morley & ?)

Note: Margaret was the daughter of Patrick Hunt of Island. Martin was the son of Austin Carney, dec'd., of (illegible).

Thomas Hunt & Honoria Godfrey
m. Feb. 1868 (William Hunt & Mary Godfrey)
Patrick, Dec. 1868 (civil record; Catherine Hunt present), Lecarrow
Mary, Jan. 1870 (Murty Hunt & Catherine Hunt; Catherine Hunt present)
Thomas, Dec. 1871 (civil record)
Austin, Feb. 1874 (civil record; Catherine Hunt of Lecarrow present)
Catherine, Dec. 1875 (civil record)
Bridget, Feb. 1877 (Michael Hunt & Bridget Hunt)
Stephen, Dec. 1878 (civil record)

John, Dec. 1881 (civil record)
Anne, Dec. 1883 (civil record)
Ellen, Oct. 1885 (civil record)
Honny, Feb. 1890 (civil record; Bridget Hunt present)

Note: Thomas, age 23, was the son of Patrick Hunt of Lecarrow. Honoria, age 20 was the daughter of Patrick Godfrey of (illegible).

David Hunt & Bridget Duffy
m. Jan. 1870 (Michael Neiland & Jane Boyle), Bekan
Thomas, Nov. 1870 (civil record), Erriff
Anne, Jan. 1872 (civil record)
Martin, July 1873 (civil record)
Michael, Sept. 1875 (civil record; Ann Duffy of Erriff present)
Bridget, Oct. 1877 (civil record; Anne Duffy of Erriff present)
Margaret Ellen, Nov. 1879 (civil record)
David, Sept. 1882 (civil record; Anne Flatley of Derrymore present)
Mary, Augt. 1884 (civil record)
John, July 1886 (civil record; Anne Hunt, sister, present)
Bridget, Feb. 1891 (civil record; Michael Hunt present)

Note: David was the son of Thomas Hunt of Coolnafarna. Bridget was the daughter of Martin Duffy of Erriff.

Margaret Hunt & Michael Connell
m. Feb. 1870 (Thomas Connell & Mary Hunt), Annagh
Mary, Jan. 1874 (John Connell & Kate Connell), Lecarrow
Catherine, Sept. 1876 (Patrick Connell & Kate Plunkett)

Note: Margaret was the daughter of Patrick Hunt of Lecarrow. Michael was the son of Michael Connell of Garraun.

Ellen Hunt & John Finnegan
m. Jan. 1871 (Bernard Malarky & Sarah Morley), Annagh

Note: Ellen was the daughter of Thomas Hunt of Leo. John was the son of James Finnegan of Tullaghaun.

Patrick Hunt & Mary Kerrane
m. Jan. 1871 (Patrick Berne & Mary Kerrane), Bekan
Thomas, Apr. 1873 (civil record), Cloonbulban, Bekan
Mary, Augt. 1877 (civil record; Sarah Kerrane of Cloonbulban present)
Bernard, Nov. 1879 (civil record; Sarah Kerrane present)
Michael, May 1882 (civil record)
Margaret, May 1882 twin (civil record)
William, Augt. 1884 (civil record)
John, Dec. 1886 (civil record)
James, Dec. 1886 twin (civil record)
Bridget, Jan. 1890 (civil record)
Kate Agnes, Oct. 1894 (civil record)

Note: Patrick was the son of Bryan Hunt, dec'd., of Bekan. Mary, age 19, was the daughter of Thomas Kerrane of Cloonbulban.

Mary Hunt & Patrick Ronayne / Ronan
m. Jan. 1871 (Michael Ronan & Bridget Regan), Kiltullagh
Patrick, Feb. 1873 (Michael Hunt & ?), Ballykillen
Mary, Augt. 1875 (Michael Hunt & Mary McWatt ?)
Honoria, Feb. 1881 (civil record)

Note: Mary, aged 25, was the daughter of Michael Hunt of Gorteen, Kiltullagh. John, age 30, was the son of John Ronayne of Ballykilleen.

Mary Hunt & Patrick Mullarky
m. March 1871 (Patrick Cunnane & Catherine Hunt), Bekan

Note: Mary was the daughter of Patrick Hunt of Larganboy. Patrick was the son of Owen Mullarky of Coolatinny, Kiltullagh.

Bridget Hunt & Thomas Fitzmaurice
m. March 1871 (Timothy Fitzmaurice & Mary McGarry), Bekan

Note: Bridget was the daughter of James Hunt of Scregg. Thomas was the son of Patrick Fitzmaurice, dec'd., of Culnacleha.

William Hunt & Mary Hunt
m. Jan. 1872 (Patrick Gildea & Rose Daly), Annagh
Bridget, Augt. 1874 (Mark Hunt & Anne Hunt), Derrynacong
John, March 1876 (John Hunt & Kate Hunt)
Catherine, March 1878 (Murty Hunt & Bridget Hunt)
Mary, March 1881 (Thomas Golden & Kate Hunt; Cecilia Hunt of Lecarrow present)
Thomas Michael, Sept. 1884 (Patrick Fitzmaurice & Mary Fitzmaurice)

Note: William was the son of Thomas Hunt, dec'd., of Derrynacong. Mary was the daughter of Murty Hunt of Lecarrow.

Honor Hunt & Bernard Brennan
Patrick, Feb. 1872 (Austin Daly & Nancy Henaghen), Culkeen, Kiltullagh

Mary Hunt & Patrick Keenan
John, Feb. 1872 (John Hunt & Ellen Hunt), Ballykillen

John Hunt & Mary Kerrane
m. Feb. 1872 (James Waldron & Mary Kerrane), Knock
Patrick, Apr. 1875 (civil record), Coolnafarna
Martin, Nov. 1877 (civil record; Bridget Kerrane of Cloonbulban present), Derryfad
Ellen, Jan. 1880 (civil record: Anne Hunt of Lecarrow present), Coolnafarna
Mary, Sept. 1881 (civil record; Bridget Hunt present)
Bridget, Oct. 1884 (civil record), Derryfad
John, Sept. 1887 (civil record), Coolnafarna

Note: John, age 24, was the son of James Hunt of Coolnafarna. Mary, age 23, was the daughter of Patrick Kerrane of Coolnafarna.

Catherine Hunt & Owen Nowlan
m. Apr. 1872 (David Nowlan & Mary Walsh), Bekan

Note: Catherine was the daughter of James Hunt, dec'd., of Larganboy. Owen was the son of Patrick Nolan, dec'd., of Belesker.

Bridget Hunt & Thomas Groarke
m. Apr. 1872 (Patrick Burke & Judith Hunt), Knock

Note: Bridget, age 25, was the daughter of William Hunt of Mannin, Aghamore Parish. Thomas, age 48 and a widower, was the son of Thomas Groarke of Mannin.

Bridget Hunt & Martin Niland
m. July 1872 (John Waldron & Honoria Caulfield), Annagh
Bridget, July 1873 (Michael ? & Bridget Regan; Honoria Hunt present), Lecarrow
Mary, March 1875 (John Niland & Bridget Niland)
Anne, Apr. 1877 (James Malloy & Sara Brennan)
Patrick, March 1879 (Martin Lyons & Anne Mulloy)

Note: no civil record of the marriage has been located.

Mary Hunt & Austin Waldron
m. Feb. 1873 (Patrick Waldron & Bridget Hunt), Bekan
Martin, July 1887 (civil record; Bridget Waldron present) Bracklaghboy

Note: Mary was the daughter of Thomas Hunt of Bracklaghboy. Austin was the son of Patrick Waldron of Bracklaghboy.

Martin Hunt & Mary Brennan
m. Apr. 1873 (Thomas Brennan & Bridget Brennan), Knock

Note: Martin was the son of Martin Hunt of Lugboy Demesne, Annagh. Mary was the daughter of James Brennan of Addergoole, Aghamore Parish.

John Hunt & Catherine Gallagher
m. Jan. 1874 (Michael Kedian & Bridget Gallagher), Kiltullagh
Mary Ann, Jan. 1875 (civil record), Brackloon
Margaret, Dec. 1877 (civil record)
John, Oct. 1881 (civil record)
James, Nov. 1886 (civil record)
Kate, Sept. 1888 (civil record; Mary Hunt present)

Note: John was the son of James Hunt, dec'd., of Brackloon. Catherine was the daughter of Thomas Gallagher of Carrick, Kiltullagh Parish.

Thomas Hunt & Catherine Lyons
m. Feb. 1874 (James Lyons & Margaret Murray), Bekan

Note: Thomas was the son of Thomas Hunt of Keebagh. Catherine was the daughter of John Lyons, dec'd., of Keebagh.

Ellen Hunt & Thomas Grealey
m. Feb. 1874 (John Healy & Bridget Lyons), Knock

Ellen, age 22, was the daughter of Thomas Hunt of Coolnafarna. Thomas, age 31, was the son of Michael Grealey of Annagh, Aghamore Parish.

Mary Hunt & John Frain
m. Feb. 1874 (Patrick Nolan & Honor Hunt), Knock

Note: Mary, age 25, was the daughter of Thomas Hunt of Balloor, Aghamore Parish. John, age 20, was rhe son of John Frain of Rath, Aghamore.

Thomas Hunt & Bridget Tierney
m. Feb. 1874 (Patrick Hunt & Margaret Hussey), Kiltullagh
Martin, Nov. 1874 (Thomas Tierney & Catherine Hunt), Mt. Devlin, Kiltullagh
Bridget, Nov. 1876 (Patrick Hett & Mary Hett; Cath. Flanagan of Mt. Devlin present)
Catherine, Jan. 1879 (Michael Hett & Bridget Hunt)

Note: Thomas was the son of Patrick Hunt of Mt. Devlin. Bridget, a widow, was the daughter of Michael Tierney of Mt. Devlin.

John Hunt & Mary Kerins / Kearns
m. March 1874 (Thomas Hunt & Anne Connell), Annagh
Catherine, Dec. 1874 (civil record), Larganboy
Honoria, Oct. 1876 (civil record)

Bridget, Feb. 1878 (civil record)
Patrick, March 1880 (civil record)
Mary, July 1881 (civil record)
Anne, Jan. 1886 (civil record)
Ellen, Apr. 1887 (civil record)
Margaret, Dec. 1888 (civil record)
Sarah, Apr. 1890 (civil record; Catherine Hunt present)
Michael, Nov. 1895 (civil record)

Note: John was the son of Patrick Hunt, dec'd., of Larganboy. Mary was the daughter of Michael Kearns of Corraun.

Mark Hunt & Bridget Murphy
m. Nov. 1874 (John Hunt & Celia Fitzmaurice),
Catherine, Nov. 1876 (Mary Murphy), Moneymore
Mary, Jan. 1878 (John Murphy & Ellen Murphy)
Philip, Oct. 1879 (civil record)
John, Nov. 1881 (civil record; John Murphy of Moneymore present)
Bridget, Dec. 1884 (civil record; Honny Fitzmaurice of Forthill present)
Michael, Oct. 1886 (civil record; Kate Hunt of Moneymore present)
Child, Oct. 1888 (civil record; Mary Hunt present)
Ellen, Dec. 1889 (civil record; Mary Anne Hunt present)

Note: Mark, age 24 (29?), was the son of Philip Hunt of Moneymore. Bridget, age 21, was the daughter of John Murphy of Treanrevagh.

Walter Hunt & Mary Toolan
m. March 1876 (Thomas Hunt & Mary Toolan), Knock
James, Feb. 1877 (civil record), Cloondace
Honoria, Dec. 1878 (civil record)
Mary Anne, Sept. 1880 (civil record; John Hunt of Cloondace present)
Thomas, May 1882 (civil record; John Hunt of Ballyhaunis present)
Margaret, June 1884 (civil record)

Note: Walter was the son of James Hunt of Cloondace, Knock Parish. Mary was the daughter of Patrick Toolan of Faughil, Knock Parish.

Austin Hunt & Bridget Moran
m. May 1876 (David Lyons & Mary Lyons), Bekan
Mary Ellen, Oct. 1877 (civil record; Margaret Moran of Clagnagh present),
Clagnagh

Note: Austin was the son of Patrick Hunt of Knockbrack. Bridget was the
daughter of John Moran of Clagnagh.

John Hunt & Catherine Hunt
Catherine, March 1877 (civil record), Reask
Honny, June 1878 (civil record)
Michael, Oct. 1883 (civil record; Margaret Hunt, sister, present)
James, June 1885 (civil record)
Ellen, Augt. 1887 (civil record, Kate Hunt present)
Anne, March 1889 (civil record)
Jane, Nov. 1891 (civil record)

Bridget Freely & John Doolan
m. March 1877 (Austin Malley & Anne Hunt), Annagh

Bridget, a widow, was the daughter of James Hunt of Knockbrack. John,
a pensioner, was the son of Walter Doolan of Ballyglass.

Patrick Hunt & Mary Keane
m. March 1878 (Patrick Regan & Bridget Keane), Kiltullagh
Bridget, Jan. 1879 (civil record), Clooncrim
Michael, Nov. 1880 (civil record; Mary Hunt of Clooncrim present)
Ellen, Jan. 1883 (civil record)
Margaret, Jan. 1885 (civil record)
Mary Anne, Dec. 1886 (civil record)
Patrick, Oct. 1889 (civil record)
Catherine, Apr. 1891 (civil record; Sarah Harkin present)
Anne, Apr. 1894 (civil record)

Note: Patrick Hunt was the son of Michael Hunt of Gorteen, Kiltullagh.
Mary Keane was the daughter of James Keane of Clooncrim.

Honoria Hunt & Michael O'Brien
m. March 1878 (John Donnelan & Catherine Hunt), Annagh
Patrick, Feb. 1879 (Thomas O'Brien & Catherine Hunt), Ballyglass / Lecarrow

Note: Honoria was the daughter of Murty Hunt of Lecarrow. Michael was the son of Michael O'Brien of Ballyglass. The civil record gave Honoria's name as Anne.

Michael Hunt & Mary McWalter
Ellen, Dec. 1878 (Patrick Hunt & Mary Hunt), Gorteen, Kiltullagh

Margaret Hunt & Michael Fox
Bartholomew Patrick, Feb. 1879 (James Finnegan & Ellen Finnegan), Leo

Bridget Hunt & Michael Royan
m. Feb. 1879 (Thomas Regan & Honora Finn), Bekan
Bridget, 1885 (Thomas Higgins & Kate Higgins)
Catherine, Nov. 1887 (civil record; Catherine Hunt present), Bracklaghboy

Note: Bridget was the daughter of Mark Hunt of Bracklaghboy. Michael was the son of Patrick Royan of Gorteen.

Patrick Hunt & Mary Finnegan
m. Feb. 1879 (Thomas Swift & Catherine Kenny), Bekan
Catherine, Nov. 1879 (civil record; Bridget Finnegan of Island present), Island
Thomas, Apr. 1881 (civil record; Bridget Finnegan of Bohogerawer present)

Note: Patrick Hunt was the son of Patrick Hunt of Island. Mary was the daughter of Thomas Finnegan of Bohogerawer.

Catherine Hunt & Patrick Concannon
m. Feb. 1879 (Maurice McWalter & Bridget Hunt), Kiltullagh

Note: Catherine, age 24, was the daughter of Patrick Hunt of Kiltobar. Patrick, age 30, was the son of Michael Concannon of Straus ?

John Hunt & Margaret Flatley
m. March 1879 (Thomas Hunt & Bridget Flatley), Annagh
Thomas, Nov. 1879 (civil record), Cloonlee
Margaret, June 1881 (civil record; Thomas Murtagh present)
John, Nov. 1884 (civil record)
Patrick, Augt. 1886 (civil record)
Bridget, Sept. 1888 (civil record)
Katie, Jan. 1895 (civil record)
James, Jan. 1896 (civil record)
Hubert, Augt. 1897 (civil record; Bridget Flatley present)
Margaret, Apr. 1899 (civil record)
William, Augt. 1900 (civil record; Ellen Morley present)

Note: John, age 23, was the son of Patrick Hunt of Cloonlee. Margaret, age 23, was the daughter of Darby Flatley of Carrow More.

Malachy Hunt & Bridget Lyons
m. March 1881 (Michael Harly & Bridget Logan), Bekan

Note: Malachy was the son of Thomas Hunt, dec'd., of Kiltacrehan ? Bridget, a widow, was the daughter of Michael Caulfield, dec'd., of Keebagh.

Michael Hunt & Mary Geraghty
m. Feb. 1882 (Patrick Regan & Margaret Kerrane), Kiltullagh
Bridget, June 1885 (civil record), Gorteen
Michael, June 1887 (civil record)
Thomas, March 1890 (civil record)
John, Oct. 1890 (civil record)
Mary, Oct. 1893 (civil record)
James, Nov. 1896 (civil record)

Note: Michael was the son of Michael Hunt of Gorteen. Mary was the daughter of Patrick Geraghty of Gorteen.

Thomas Hunt & Margaret Fitzmaurice
m. Feb. 1882 (John Hunt & Honoria Fitzmaurice), Bekan

Note: John was the son of John Hunt of Cloonbook. Margaret was the daughter of Thomas Fitzmaurice of Brackloon.

Ellen Hunt & John Prenty
m. March 1882 (John Waldron & Mary Rogers), Annagh
John Arthur, Oct. 1884 (civil record), Tooraree
Bridget Ellen, Augt. 1886 (civil record)
Honoria, Augt. 1886 twin (civil record)
Agatha Elizabeth, Feb. 1893 (civil record)
Rose Agnes, Jan. 1895 (civil record; Annie Prenty present)

Note: Ellen was the daughter of James Hunt of Derrynacong. John was the son of Arthur Prenty of Tooraree. Civil record recorded the witness's name as Winifred Rogers. Ellen Prenty died in May 1903.

Thomas Hunt & Margaret Kearns / Kerins
m. March 1882 (John Hunt & Bridget Kearns), Knock
Mary Ellen, Augt. 1883 (civil record; Mary Kearns grandmother present), Buladurris ?
Honny, Dec. 1884 (civil record)
James, Oct. 1887 (civil record)
Maggie, Augt. 1889 (civil record)
John, Oct. 1891 (civil record)
Bridget, Jan. 1894 (civil record)
Katie, March 1897 (civil record; Mary Kearns present), Carrownamallaght, Knock

Note: Thomas was the son of James Hunt of Cloonease ? Margaret was the daughter of James Kearns of Carrownamallaght, Knock.

William Hunt & Mary Morley
m. Feb. 1883 (Luke Morley & Ellen Morley), Knock
William, Dec. 1883 (civil record; Mary Greeley of Bekan present), Coolnafarna
Mary, Apr. 1885 (civil record)
Margaret, Apr. 1887 (civil record)
Celia, Apr. 1890 (civil record; Luke Morley present)
John, June 1892 (civil record)

Bridget, Dec. 1894 (civil record)
Luke, March 1897 (civil record; Celia Murray present)
Ellen, March 1897 twin (civil record)
Martin, Nov. 1899 (civil record)

Note: William, age 25, was the son of William Hunt of Coolnafarna.
Mary, age 22, was the daughter of Luke Morley of Coolnafarna.

Thomas Hunt & Mary Regan
m. Feb. 1884 (James Hunt & Julia Grogan), Annagh
John, Jan. 1885 (John Regan & Mary Anne Kenny), Derrynacong
Honoria, Dec. 1885 (? Hunt & Mary Regan)
Michael Francis, Sept. 1887 (Francis Regan & Mary Kelly; John Regan
present)
Thomas, Augt. 1891 (Michael Regan & Mary Regan)

Note: Thomas was the son of James Hunt of Derrynacong. Mary was the
daughter of Patrick Regan of Killunaugher.

Julia Hunt & Patrick Finn
m. March 1884 (Michael Mulkeen & Margaret Mulkeen), Bekan

Note: Julia was the daughter of John Hunt, dec'd., of Cloonbook. Patrick
was the son of James Finn of Loqilla, Mayo ?

Anne Hunt & Anthony Rattigan
m. March 1884 (Michael Eagan & Catherine Kedian), Bekan

Note: Anne was the daughter of William Hunt of Cloonbook. Anthony
was the son of Patrick Rattigan, dec'd., of Coogue.

Mary Hunt & Thomas Forde
m. May 1884 (Michael Tully & Kate Fitzmaurice) Kiltullagh
Bridget, Jan. 1888 (Hugh Hunt & Maggie Tully), Derrynacong
Mary Ellen, May 1889 (James Waldron & Kate Waldron)
Patrick, Augt. 1892 (Patrick Fitzmaurice & Bridget Fitzmaurice)
Kate, Dec.1893 (Michael Hunt & Mary Fitzmaurice)

Delia, Dec. 1893 twin (Patrick Tully & Mary Waldron)
John, Jan. 1896 (John Waldron & Delia ? Waldron)

Note: Mary the daughter of Patrick Hunt & Bridget Fitzmaurice of Laughil, Kiltullagh. Thomas Forde was the son of Patrick Forde & Bridget Freeman of Derrynacong.

Catherine Hunt & Patrick Kelly
m. Oct. 1885 (William Mitchel & Mary McDonagh), Annagh

Note: Catherine was the daughter of Murty Hunt of Lecarrow. Patrick was the son of Peter Kelly of Cloonagh. County Galway.

Eleanor Hunt & Hugh Kearney
m. Jan. 1886 (John Kearney & Margaret Hunt), Bekan

Note: Eleanor was the daughter of James Hunt, dec'd., of Bekan townland. Hugh was the son of John Kearney of Carrowkeel.

Margaret Hunt & Peter Connelly
m. Feb. 1887 (John Mannion & Mary Anne Waldron), Bekan

Note: Margaret, a widow, was the daughter of Thomas Fitzmaurice of Cloonbook. Peter was the son of James Connelly of Clooncrim.

Bridget Hunt & Thomas Gallagher
m. March 1887 (Patrick Regan & Margaret Hunt), Annagh

Note: Bridget was the daughter of Laurence Hunt, dec'd., of Knockanarra. Thomas was the son of Thomas Gallagher of Ballykenane ?

Catherine Hunt & Michael Shaughnessy
m. Feb. 1888 (John Shaughnessy & Anne Hunt), Kiltullagh

Note: Catherine, a widow (nee Concannon), was the daughter of Patrick Hunt of Streamstown ? Michael was the son of Michael Shaughnessy of Cloonfad Upper.

Patrick Hunt & Bridget Ruane
m. Feb. 1888 (Austin Healy & Maggie Gallagher), Bekan
Margaret, Dec. 1889 (civil record) Knockanarra
Patrick, Apr. 1895 (civil record; Matthew Waldron, cousin, present)
Mary, Jan. 1898 (civil record)

Note: Patrick was the son of Laurence Hunt, dec'd., of Knockanarra.
Bridget was the daughter of John Ruane, dec'd., of Johnstown ?

Ellen Hunt & Francis Helbert
m. May 1888 (John Morris & Mary Fitzmaurice), Bekan

Note: Ellen, age 21, was the daughter of James Hunt of Ballinvilla, Bekan.
Francis, age 23, was the son of William Helbert of Lecarrow.

James Hunt & Margaret McHale
m. March 1889 (Owen Eagen & Mary Mullaney), Knock
Mary Anne, Feb. 1890 (civil record; Anne McHale present), Cloonlee,
Knock
Honoria, Oct. 1891 (civil record)
James, Jan. 1893 (civil record)
Bridget, Augt. 1894 (civil record)
Thomas, Nov. 1895 (civil record)
Julia, Nov. 1899 (civil record; Mary Anne Hunt present)
John, Nov. 1901 (civil record; Mary Anne Hunt present)

Note: James, age 31, was the son of James Hunt, Cloondace. Margaret, age
20, was the daughter of William McHale of Cloonice ?

John Hunt & Elizabeth Loftus
m. Feb. 1890 (John Hunt & Bridget Costello), Kiltullagh

Note: John was the son of Murty Hunt of Lecarrow. Elizabeth was the
daughter of James Loftus of Grange, Kiltullagh.

Michael Hunt & Bridget Ganley
m. Feb. 1890 (Thomas Fitzmaurice & Kate Ganley), Loughglynn

Patrick Joseph, Dec. 1890 (Patrick Hunt & Catherine Waldron), Tully, Tibohine Parish
Mary, July 1892 (Edward Quinn & Mary Flanagan)
Dominick, Jan. 1894 (Patrick Waldron & Bridget Waldron)
Catherine, Dec. 1896 (John McNulty & Catherine Ganley)
Rose Ann, Dec. 1900 (civil record)
Bridget Agnes, Dec. 1900 twin (civil record)
Michael, March 1904 (civil record)
Margaret, Jan. 1908 (civil record)
Josephine, June 1912, (civil record), Milltown, Baslick Parish

Note: Michael, age 24, was the son of Patrick Hunt & Bridget Fitzmaurice of Laughil. Bridget, age 19, was the daughter of Dominick Ganley & Catherine McNulty of Tully, County Roscommon.

Mary Hunt & Martin Moran
m. Augt. 1891 (Thomas Mullarky & Bridget Hunt), Bekan

Note: Mary was the daughter of John Hunt of Bracklaghboy. Martin was the son of John Moran of Coolesker ?

Patrick Hunt & Celia Hussey
m. Feb. 1892 (Nicholas Hussey & Ellen Hussey), Kiltullagh
Bridget, Nov. 1892 (Thomas Hussey & Ellen Hussey)
Patrick, Dec. 1893 (Andrew Corr & Mary Fitzmaurice)
Mary Anne, Sept. 1895 (Michael Hussey & Catherine Winston)
Andrew, Sept. 1897 (Austin Winston & Bridget Casserly)
Catherine, Jan. 1899 (James Kilraine & Catherine Kilraine)
Maggie, Dec. 1901 (civil record)

Note: Patrick was the son of Patrick Hunt & Bridget Fitzmaurice of Laughil. Celia Hussey was from Clydagh, Kiltullagh. The civil marriage record has not been located.

John Hunt & Bridget Flatley
m. March 1894 (James McLoughlin & Margaret Boyle), Knock
Honny, June 1895 (civil record), Ballyhaunis

John William, June 1896 (civil record)
Delia Mary, March 1898 (civil record), Wingfield ?
William Patrick, May 1900 (civil record)
James Joseph, May 1900 twin (civil record)

Note: John, a widower and shopkeeper, was the son of Patrick Hunt of Cloonlee. Bridget was the daughter of Hugh Flatley of Cloonlee. Bridget's name was given as Maggie in the marriage record.

Thomas Hunt & Mary Mulkeen
m. Dec. 1895 (John Conway & Nora Mulkeen), Bekan

Note: the civil marriage record has not been located.

Thomas Hunt & Mary Clynes
m. Dec. 1895 (John Conway & Nora Clynes), Annagh

Note: Thomas, age 26, was the son of William Hunt of Killknock. Mary, age 21, was the daughter of James Clynes of Carrow More.

Thomas Hunt & Anne Boland
m. March 1896 (William Forde & Kate Cox), Annagh
Patrick, Nov. 1896 (John Hunt & Mary Hunt), Derrynacong
John, Jan. 1898 (Thomas Hunt & Mary Hunt)
Kate, Dec. 1899 (Thomas Kilfoyle & Anne Caulfield)
Bridget, Augt. 1903 (William Boland & Mary Fitzmaurice)
Anne, Oct. 1906 (Patrick McGuire & Kate McGuire)

Note: Thomas was the son of John Hunt of Reask. Anne was the daughter of Patrick Boland & Bridget McGuire of Derrynacong.

Thomas Hunt & Norah Kelly
m. Feb. 1897 (James Finnegan & Norah Gallagher), Annagh
Mary, Jan. 1899 (civil record), Tullaghaun
Patrick, Feb. 1901 (civil record)
Thomas, Oct. 1903 (civil record)

Note: Thomas, age 28, was the son of Thomas Hunt of Corrasluastia. Norah, age 27, was the daughter of Patrick Kelly of Tullaghaun.

John Hunt & Bridget Higgins
m. March 1897 (Martin Hunt & Minnie Burke), Kiltullagh
Mary, Feb. 1898 (civil record) Pollanalty
Bridget, March 1901 (civil record)

Note: John, age 35, was the son of Patrick Hunt of Kiltobar. Bridget, age 29, was the daughter of Michael Higgins of Kiltobar.

John Hunt & Bridget Kelly
m. July 1897 (Thomas Flynn & Bridget Moran), Annagh

Note: John, age 28 & a R.I.C. constable, was the son of Patrick Hunt, dec'd., of Bunnadober. Bridget, age 32, a teacher and a widow, was the daughter of Timothy Flynn of Lugboy Demesne.

James Hunt & Teresa Hennessy
m. Nov. 1897 (Patrick Mooney & Anna Marie Cavanagh), Granard Union, Longford
John James Augustine, Augt. 1899 (civil record; Biddy Costello present), Ballyhaunis

Note: James was an R.I.C. constable, the son of Bartl. Hunt, dec'd., of Ballina. Teresa was the daughter of Thomas Hennessy, dec'd. of Drumul.

Delia Hunt & Luke Tighe
m. Feb. 1898 (? Higgins & Anne Hunt), Annagh

Note: Delia, age 26, was the daughter of Patrick Hunt of Lecarrow. Luke was the son of Michael Tighe of Coltucrehen ?

Bridget Hunt & John Grogan
m. March 1898 (John Walsh & Anne Walsh), Bekan
Child, March 1901 (civil record), Killunaugher

Note: Bridget, age 21, was the daughter of John Hunt of Bracklaghboy. John, age 30, was the son of Michael Grogan of Killunaugher.

John Hunt & Margaret Judge
m. Apr. 1898 (William Hunt & Mary Judge), Annagh
Bridget, Feb. 1899 (civil record), Lecarrow
Mary, Oct. 1900 (civil record)
Murty, Nov. 1901 (civil record; Bridget Hunt, grandmother, present)

Note: John was the son of Murty Hunt of Lecarrow. Margaret was the daughter of Thomas Judge of Lecarrow.

Honoria Hunt & Thomas Burke
m. Feb. 1900 (Peter Burke & Mary A. Hunt), Knock

Note: Honoria was the daughter of Walter Hunt of Cloondace. Thomas was the son of Michael Burke of Mace ?

Thomas Hunt & Mary Anne Ryan
James, March 1900 (civil record), Scregg
Patrick, Feb. 1901 (civil record)

Note: the civil marriage record has not been located.

Mary Ann Hunt & Michael Mullanny
m. March 1900 (Patrick Mullanny & Kate Hunt), Bekan

Note: Mary Ann was the daughter of Thomas Hunt of Keebagh. Michael was the son of Patrick Mullanay of Meelick, Kiltullagh.

John Hunt & Ellen Lyons
m. May 1900 (John Lyons & Bridget Kilfoyle), Bekan

Note: John was the son of Thomas Hunt of Cuiltycreaghan. Ellen was the daughter of Thomas Lyons of Greenwood.

Winnie Hunt & John Moran
Mary, Augt. 1900 (civil record), Ballyhaunis

Note: the marriage record has not been located.

Bridget Hunt & Patrick Lyons
m. Oct. 1900 (Martin Higgins & Mary Hunt), Annagh

Note: Bridget was the daughter of William and Mary Hunt of Derrynacong. Patrick was the son of Patrick Lyons of Brackloon.

Ellen Hunt & John Diviney
m. Augt. 1901 (Patrick Conway & Molly Hunt), Knock

Note: Ellen was the daughter of John Hunt of Coolnafarna. John was the son of Owen Diviny of Barnacarroll, Kilcolman Parish, Mayo.

Catherine Hunt & Patrick Glavey
m. Feb. 1902 (John Waldron & Eleanor Florence Hunt), Annagh

Note: Catherine was the daughter of William and Mary Hunt of Derrynacong. Patrick was the son of Thady Glavey of Aghamore Parish.

Nora Hunt & Peter Fitzmaurice
m. May 1902 (Michael Fitzmaurice & Lizzie Hunt), Annagh

Note: Nora was the daughter of James Hunt of Scregg. Peter was the son of Michael Fitzmaurice of Forthill.

M. Hunt & Thomas Murray
m. June 1902 (Kate Barnicle), Bekan

Note: the marriage record has not been located.

Mary Hunt & Patrick Nolan
m. Feb. 1903 (James Fahy & Ellen Nolan), Bekan

Note: Mary was the daughter of Thomas Hunt of Cuiltycreaghan. Patrick was the son of Patrick Nolan of Larganboy.

Bridget Hunt & John Biesty
m. Apr. 1903 (Patrick Fitzmaurice & Kate Hunt), Bekan

Note: Bridget was the daughter of Darby Hunt of Cuiltycreaghan. John was the son of Edward Biesty of Pattenspark.

James Hunt & Bridget McGrath
m. May 1904 (James Fitzmaurice & Delia Waldron), Annagh

Note: James was the son of James Hunt of Scregg. Bridget was the daughter of Michael McGrath of Drumnaderry.

Mary Ellen Hunt & James Kenny
m. Feb. 1906 (Joseph Hunt & Rita Spelman), Annagh
James, Apr. 1907 (Thomas Hunt & Nora Tighe), Derrynacong
Mary, June 1908 (Michael Tighe & Nora Tighe)

Note: Mary Ellen was the daughter of Patrick Hunt of Lecarrow. James was the son of Patrick Kenny of Derrynacong.

William Hunt & Nora Dyer
m. March 1906 (James Waldron & Delia Dyer), Bekan

Note: William was the son of William Hunt of Cloonbook. Nora was the daughter of Patrick Dyer of Brackloon.

Ellen Hunt & Michael Kenny
m. March 1906 (Michael Finn & Katie Hunt), Bekan

Note: Ellen was the daughter of John Hunt of Clagnagh. Michael was the son of Martin Kenny of Erriff.

Mary J. Hunt & David Jordan
m. Apr. 1907 (Michael Ganly & Norah Hunt), Annagh

Note: Mary was the daughter of Patrick Hunt, dec'd., of Lecarrow. David was the son of Dominick Jordan of Lecarrow.

Mary Hunt & Thomas Loftus
m. Jan. 1908 (John Hunt & Maggie Flanagan), Loughglynn

Note: Mary was the daughter of Michael Hunt of Ballyglass West. Thomas was the son of John Loftus of Meelick.

Martin Hunt & Delia Murphy
m. March 1908 (Patrick Cooney & Jane Smyth ?), Knock

Note: Martin was the son of John Hunt of Derradda, Knock. Delia was the daughter of Michael Murphy of Gorteen and Coolnafarna.

Katherine Hunt & John A. Prenty
m. Augt. 1908 (John Hunt & Agatha Prenty), Annagh

Katherine was the daughter of Mark Hunt of Moneymore. John, a widower, was the son of Arthur Prenty of Tooraree.

Mary A. Hunt & Patrick Boyle
m. Dec. 1908 (Richard Stanton & Mary Boyle), Bekan

Note: Mary, age 35, was the daughter of Darby Hunt of Cuiltycreaghan. Patrick, age 30, was the son of James Boyle of Cuiltycreaghan.

Mary Hunt & Edward Johnston
m. Apr. 1909 (Thomas Johnston & Maggie Hunt), Bekan

Note: Mary was the daughter of John Hunt of Larganboy West. Edward, an egg merchant, was the son of Thomas Johnston of Reask.

Nellie Hunt & James Cruise
m. Jan. 1910 (Joseph Cruise & Margaret Jordan), Annagh

Note: Nellie was the daughter of Thomas Hunt of Lecarrow. James was the son of Thomas Cruise of Knockbrack.

Thomas Hunt & Mary O'Donnell
m. March 1910 (Patrick Waldron & Annie O'Donnell), Bekan

Note: Thomas was the son of John Hunt, dec'd., of Brackloon South. Mary was the daughter of Andrew O'Donnell, dec'd., of Tawnaghmore.

Michael Hunt & Bridget Grogan
Mark, Jan. 1912 (civil record), Moneymore

Note: the marriage record has not been located.

Thomas Hunt & Bridget Stenson
m. Apr. 1912 (Edward Boyle & Anne Stenson), Aghamore
Margaret, March 1913 (civil record) Island
Patrick, July 1914 (civil record)
Thomas, Sept. 1915 (civil record)

Note: Thomas was the son of Patrick Hunt of Island. Bridget was the daughter of Thomas Stenson, dec'd., of Ballinclougha ?

Anne Hunt & James Fitzmaurice
m. Apr. 1913 (Thomas Fitzmaurice & Margaret Hunt), Bekan

Note: Anne, age 27, was the daughter of John Hunt of Larganboy. James, age 28, was the son of Michael Fitzmaurice of Spaddagh.

Anne Hunt & Patrick Freely
m. Nov. 1913 (John Thomas Freely & Mary Dillon), Annagh
Jerome, June 1916 (Peter Freely & M. Kenny), Derrynacong
John, Sept. 1918 (Michael Tighe & Anne Tighe)
Patrick, March 1922 (Luke Tighe & Delia Tighe)

Anne was the daughter of Patrick Hunt of Lecarrow. Patrick was the son of John Freely of Derrynacong.

Patrick Hunt & Ellen Morley
m. March 1914 (James Hunt & Mary Anne McLoughlin), Knock

Note: Patrick, age 40, was the son of Patrick Hunt of Brackloon. Ellen, age 31, was the daughter of John Morley of Lugboy Demesne.

Patrick Hunt & Mary Walsh
m. July 1915 (John Cunnane & Anne Walsh), Annagh

Note: Patrick, age 34, was the son of John Hunt of Larganboy. Mary, age 18, was the daughter of Michael Walsh of Drumnaderry

Katie Hunt & Eugene Conway
m. May 1916 (Patrick Duggan & Bridget Mullaney), Bekan

Note: Katie, age 27, was the daughter of Thomas Hunt of Keebagh. Eugene, age 30, was the son of John Conway of Carrow Beg.

James Hunt & Mary Haugh
m. Oct. 1916 (John Hunt & Kate Farrell), Ballyhaunis

Note: James, a policeman, was the son of James Hunt of Hollymount. Mary, age 19, was the daughter of Patrick Haugh, shopkeeper, of Ballyhaunis.

Celia Hunt & Daniel Murray
m. Feb. 1917 (James Murray & Katie Hunt), Annagh

Note: Celia, age 27, was the daughter of William Hunt of Coolnafarna. Daniel, age 37, was the son of William Murray of Lissaniska.

Katie Hunt & Peter Lynch
m. June 1917 (George Amos ? & Ellie Hough), Claremorris Church

Note: Katie, age, 24, was the daughter of Patrick Hunt of Bracklagh. Peter, age 31, was the son of Peter Lynch of Killucan.

Ellen Hunt & John Waldron
m. March 1918 (Thomas Waldron & Margaret Fitzmaurice), Bekan

Note: Ellen, age 30, was the daughter of John Hunt of Reask. John, age 36 and a widower, was the son of Patrick Waldron of Brackloon.

John Hunt & Ellen Grogan
m. Apr. 1918 (Martin Hunt & Delia Kenny), Bekan

Note: John, age 28, was the son of John Hunt of Derryfad. Ellen, age 27, was the daughter of Martin Grogan of Bekan townland.

Margaret Hunt & John Fergus
m. July 1918 (Thomas Morrison & Julia Mulkeen), Bekan

Note: Margaret, age 32, was the daughter of Patrick Hunt of Bracklagh. John, age 27, was the son of Martin Fergus of Cloontumper.

Ellen Waldron & Peter Freeley
m. Nov. 1919 (Joseph Freeley & Katie Hunt), Bekan

Note: Ellen, a widow, was the daughter of John Hunt of Brackloon. Peter was the son of John Freeley of Brackloon.

James Hunt & Rose Anne Morris
m. March 1920 (Patrick Hunt & Nora Johnston), Bekan

Note: James was the son of John Hunt of Reask. Rose Anne was the daughter of Patrick Morris of Kilgarriff, Aghamore.

Mary Hunt & Michael Malia
m. March 1920 (Patrick Folliard & Bridget Hunt), Annagh

Note: Mary, age 20, was the daughter of James Hunt of Lecarrow. Michael was the son of Patt Malia of Grange.

Thomas Hunt & Ellen Prendergast
m. Apr. 1921 (Patrick Mullaney & Rose Prendergast), Bekan

Note: Thomas, age 35 ?, was the son of Thomas Hunt of Keebagh. Ellen, age 19, was the daughter of Michael Prendergast of Reask.

John Hunt & Margaret McHugh
m. May 1922 (Martin Hunt & Mary Kate Boyle), Annagh

Note: John was the son of William Hunt of Coolnafarna. Margaret was the daughter of Hugh McHugh of Coolnafarna.

Catherine Hunt & Thomas Boyle
m. June 1923 (Peter Boyle & Mary Anne Keane), Kiltullagh

Note: Catherine was the daughter of Patrick Hunt of Clooncrim. Thomas, age 27, was the son of Austin Boyle of Cashel.

Delia Hunt & Michael Rogers
m. Nov. 1923 (Frank Walsh & Kate McCormack), Kiltullagh

Note: Delia, age 33, was the daughter of Michael Hunt of Gorteen. Michael, age 30, was the son of Patrick Rogers of Castlequarter.

Ellen Hunt & Thomas Hanlon
m. Apr. 1924 (Vincent Kelly & Kathleen Keane), Kiltullagh

Note: Ellen was the daughter of Patrick Hunt of Clooncrim. Thomas, age 38, was the son of Patrick Hanlon of Carrick.

Mary Hunt & Francis Kelly
m. May 1925 (James Quinn & Nellie Finnegan), Annagh

Note: Mary was the daughter of Thomas Hunt of Tullaghaun. Francis was the son of Patrick Kelly of Ballinlough.

Anne Hunt & James Casserly
m. July 1925 (John Hussey & Catherine Garrity), Kiltullagh
Note: Anne, age 30, was the daughter of Patrick Hunt of Clooncrim.
James, age 33, was the son of Andrew Casserly of Clydagh.

Mary Hunt & John Rush
m. Nov. 1925 (John Keane & Bridget Geraghty), Kiltullagh

Note: Mary, age 37, was the daughter of Patrick Hunt of Clooncrim. John,
age 40, was the son of Dominick Rush of Clooncrim.

Bridget Agnes Hunt & John Thomas Fitzmaurice
m. March 1926 (Dominick Fitzmaurice & Margaret Hunt), Loughglynn

Note: Bridget Agnes was the daughter of Michael Hunt & Bridget Ganley
of Tully. John was the son of Andrew Fitzmaurice & Bridget Flatley of
Brackloon.

John T. Hunt & Mary K. Coen
m. June 1926 (Dominick Jordan & Rita ? McDonnell), Annagh

Note: John was the son of Patrick Hunt of Lecarrow. Mary was the
daughter of Thomas Coen of Lecarrow.

Michael Hunt & Anna Ganley
m. June 1926 (Edmond Morley & Jennie Ganley), Annagh

Note: Michael was the son of Thomas J. Hunt of Derrynacong. Anna was
the daughter of Thomas Ganley of Derrynacong.

Catherine Hunt & John Thomas Heneghan
m. Apr. 1929 (Thomas Mullarkey & Sarah Murphy), Annagh

Note: Catherine was the daughter of Thomas Hunt of Derrynacong. John
was the son of Patrick Heneghan of Lisduff.

Walter Hunt & Bridget Waldron

m. Nov. 1929 (John Hughes & Josephine Waldron)

Note: Walter was the son of John Hunt, dec'd., of Barnacarroll, Kilcolman Parish. Bridget was the daughter of Luke Waldron of Cloonbook.

Catherine Hunt & John Reynolds
m. June 1931 (Parick Finan & Anna Hunt), Kiltullagh

Note: Catherine was the daughter of John Hunt of Kiltobar. John was the son of William Reynolds of Meelick.

Martin Hunt & Nellie Murphy
m. Sept. 1931 (Martin Grogan & Anne Lynch), Annagh

Note: Martin was the son of William Hunt of Coolnafarna. Nellie was the daughter of John Murphy of Coolnafarna.

Kate Hunt & John Murphy
m. Oct. 1931 (Joseph McDonagh & Mary Hunt), Annagh

Note: Kate was the daughter of William Hunt of Coolnafarna. John was the son of John Murphy of Coolnafarna.

John Hunt & Mary Carroll
m. March 1933 (Michael Cronin & Eileen Cruise), Annagh

Note: John was the son of John Hunt of Lecarrow. Mary was the daughter of Thomas Carroll of Knockbrack.

Thomas Hunt & Mary Kate Rogers
m. July 1933 (Patrick Finnegan & Rose Rogers), Kiltullagh

Note: Thomas was the son of Thomas Hunt of Tullaghaun. Mary Kate was the daughter of Michael Rogers of Lisnagroob, Kiltullagh.

Mary Catherine Hunt & John McGovern
m. Augt. 1934 (Patrick Grogan & Catherine Hussey), Kiltullagh

Note: Mary Catherine was the son of Michael Hunt of Gorteen. John, a widower, was the son of Thomas McGovern of Ardaragh ?

Michael Hunt & Margaret Hett
m. Apr. 1936 (Thomas Hunt & Anne Hett), Kiltullagh

Note: Thomas, age 29, was the son of John Hunt of Kiltobar. Margaret, age 28, was the daughter of Thomas Hett of Kiltobar.

John Hunt & Elizabeth Moloney
m. Nov. 1936 (Joseph Regan & Margaret Caulfield), Annagh

Note: John, age 32, was the son of Thomas Hunt of Brackloon. Elizabeth, age 25, was the daughter of Patrick Moloney of Derrynacong.

Hunt – Civil Death of Records (informants in parentheses)

Hugh Hunt, 1865, 65, Derrymore
Bridget Hunt, Apr. 1871, 58, widow, Larganboy (Catherine Hunt)
Margaret Hunt, Apr. 1871, 40, married, in childbirth, Knockanarra (Bridget Hunt)
Bridget Hunt, June 1871, 78, widow, Derrymore (Walter Waldron)
Thomas Hunt, Dec. 1871, 2, Laughil (Ellen Disken of Corrasluastia)
Child Hunt, Jan. 1872, 2 months, Reask (John Hunt)
Honoria Hunt, Feb. 1872, 2, Bracklaghboy (Anne Hunt)
Bridget Hunt, Dec. 1872, 60, widow, Cloonfad (John Hunt of Cloonfad)
Patrick Hunt, Dec. 1872, 70, widower, Larganboy (Catherine Hunt)
Ellen Hunt, May 1873, 2, Lecarrow (Catherine Cribbin of Lecarrow)
John Hunt, Sept. 1873, 7 weeks, Reask (Honoria Ford of Reask)
Philip Hunt, Feb. 1874, 72, widower, Moneymore (Mark Hunt of Moneymore)
Thomas Hunt, Feb. 1874, 71, married, Lecarrow (Michael Murphy)
Austin Hunt, Augt. 1874, 6 months, Lecarrow (Thomas Hunt)
Michael Hunt, Oct. 1874, 6 months, Bekan (Michael Hunt)
Michael John Hunt, Nov. 1874, 5 months, Bekan (Michael Hunt)
Thomas Hunt, Feb. 1875, 65, widower, Coolnafarna (Bridget Hunt)
Bridget Hunt, June 1875, 8, Bekan (Mary Hunt)

John Hunt, July 1875, 71, widower, Cloonbook (Julia Hunt)

Catherine Hunt, Augt. 1875, 42, married, Reask (Margaret Doogan of Reask)

Catherine Hunt, Augt. 1875, 2, Bracklaghboy (Anne Hunt)

Catherine Hunt, Apr. 1876, 5 months, Lecarrow (Catherine Hunt)

John Hunt, Augt. 1876, 30, married, Bracklaghboy (Anne Hunt)

Thomas Hunt, Oct. 1876, 6, Erriff (Bridget Hunt)

Patrick Hunt, Nov. 1876, 29, single, Lecarrow (Mary Niland of Lecarrow)

James Hunt, Jan. 1877, 78, married, Cloondace (Honoria Hunt)

Anne Hunt, Feb. 1877, 1, Reask (John Hunt)

Honoria Hunt, March 1877, 56, widow, Cloondace (Walter Hunt)

Michael Hunt, May 1877, 18, Bracklaghboy (Honoria Hunt)

Mary Hunt, Sept. 1877, 65, widow, Lisbaun (Mary Finn)

Mary Hunt, Jan. 1879, 30, married, Gorteen (Patrick Hunt of Clooncrim)

James Hunt, July 1879, 58, married, Bekan (Margaret Hunt)

Child Hunt, Sept. 1879, 1 day, Lecarrow (Bridget Hunt)

Mark Hunt, Oct. 1879, 60, married, Bracklaghboy (Honoria Hunt)

Patrick Hunt, Nov. 1879, 24, single, Bekan (Margaret Hunt)

Catherine Hunt, Nov. 1879, 60, widow, Lecarrow (Patrick Hunt)

Anne Hunt, Nov. 1879, 3 days, Lecarrow (Patrick Hunt)

Mark Hunt, March 1880, 52, single, Lecarrow (Bridget McGrath)

Mary Hunt, Apr. 1880, 70, widow, Killunaugher (Margaret Waldron)

Thomas Hunt, June 1880, 56, widower, Reask (John Hunt)

Austin Hunt, July 1880, 22, single, Cloonbookoughter (Julia Hunt)

Bridget Hunt, July 1880, 70, widow, Churchfield (Michael Tigue)

Thomas Hunt, Dec. 1880, 60, married, Killunaugher (Bridget Hunt)

James Hunt, May 1881, 8, Coolnafarna (Catherine Waldron)

Honoria Hunt, Nov. 1882, 56, married, Derrynacong (Thomas Hunt, son)

Catherine Hunt, Jan. 1883, 26, single, Scregg (Thomas Hunt, brother)

Michael Hunt, March 1884, 85, married, Gorteen (Patrick Hunt, son, of Clooncrim)

Michael Austin Hunt, March 1884, 3, Clooncrim (Patrick Hunt, father)

Anne Hunt, March 1884, 3 months, Lecarrow (Mary Hunt, mother)

Patrick Hunt, Apr. 1884, 53, married, Laughil (Catherine Fitzmaurice)

William Hunt, Apr. 1884, 77, married, Cloonfad (John Prendergast of Mace ?)

Murtagh Hunt, Dec. 1884, 52, Lecarrow (Bridget Hunt, wife)

Thomas Hunt, Jan. 1885, 68, married, Leo (Ellen Finnegan, daughter)

Mary Hunt, Jan. 1885, 27, married, Cloondace (John Hunt of Ballyhaunis)

Sarah Hunt, Jan. 1885, 70, single, (Claremorris Workhouse)

Mary Hunt, March 1885, 89, widow, Bekan (John Hunt, grandson)

Sarah Hunt, May 1885, 63, widow, Bekan (Ellen Hunt, daughter)

Thomas Hunt, Nov. 1885, 25, married, Cloonbookoughter (Honny Fitzmaurice)

Michael James Hunt, Nov. 1885, 6 months, Clooncrim (Patrick Hunt, father)

Margaret Hunt, Feb. 1887, 66, widow, Brackloon (Catherine Hunt, daughter)

Thomas Hunt, June 1887, 80, widower, Bracklaghboy (James Hunt, son)

Malachy Hunt, July 1887, 65, widower, Knockanarra (Patrick Hunt, son)

Bridget Hunt, Augt. 1887, 10, Erriff (Catherine Culkeen of Erriff)

Patrick Hunt, Feb. 1888, 19, Reask (Kate Hunt, stepsister)

Cicely Hunt, March 1888, 74, widow, Lecarrow (Patrick Tarpey)

Child Hunt, Oct. 1888, 1 day, Moneymore (Mary Hunt, sister)

Ellen Hunt, Augt. 1889, 86, widow, Gorteen (Mary Hunt, daughter-in-law)

Nancy Hunt, Oct. 1889, 80, widow, Lecarrow (Celia Hunt, sister-in-law)

Bridget Hunt, June 1890, 70, widow, Derryfad (Mary Costello, cousin)

Margaret Hunt, Augt. 1891, 39, Cloonlee (John Hunt, husband)

Walter Hunt, Oct. 1891, 47, widower, Cloondace (Margaret Hunt, sister-in-law)

Michael William Hunt, Dec. 1891, 7, Killunaugher (William Kelly, uncle)

Anne Hunt, March 1893, 65, Knockbrack (James Hunt, husband)

Delia Hunt, Augt. 1893, 9, Derryfad (Catherine Waldron, aunt)

James Hunt, Nov. 1893, 90, widower, Kiltobar (Patrick Brennan)

Ellen Hunt, March 1894, 5, Coolnafarna (William Hunt, father)

Anne Hunt, March 1895, 65, widow, Bracklaghboy (Bridget Hunt, daughter)

Honny Hunt, Sept. 1895, 3 months, Ballyhaunis (John Hunt, father)

Patrick Hunt, Oct. 1895, 69, widower, Clagnagh (John Hunt, son)

Patrick Hunt, March 1896, 94, Island (Margaret Hunt, wife)

James Hunt, Feb. 1897, 70, widower, Derrynacong (Mary Hunt, daughter-in-law)

Murty Hunt, Apr. 1897, 82, married, Lecarrow (John Hunt, son)

James Hunt, June 1897, 70, married, Scregg (Mary Hunt, daughter-in-law)

Thomas Hunt, June 1897, 45, Carhoon-a-nanagh ? (Margaret Hunt, wife)

William Hunt, Sept. 1897, 66, married, Cloonbookoughter (Honny Hunt, daughter)

Mary Hunt, March 1898, 12 days, Pollanalty (Delia Hunt, mother)

Norah Hunt, Jan. 1898, 50, Clagnagh (John Hunt, husband)

Kate Hunt, July 1898, 16 months, Ballydorris ? (Margaret Hunt, mother)

Catherine Hunt, Dec. 1898, 63, widow, Leo (Mary Finnegan, granddaughter)

William Patrick Hunt, July 1900, 6 weeks, Wingfield (Bridget Hunt, mother)

James Joseph Hunt, July 1900, 6 weeks, Wingfield (Bridget Hunt, mother)

Celia Hunt, July 1901, 89, widow, Lecarrow (John Hunt, son)

Ellen Hunt, Feb. 1904, 14, Moneymore (Mark Hunt)

John Hunt, May 1904, 19, Derrynacong (Annie Hunt, cousin)

Bridget Hunt, Nov. 1906, 80, widow, Pollanalty (John Hunt, son)

Bridget Hunt, March 1907, 81, widow, Killunaugher (John Hunt, son)

Bridget Hunt, Feb. 1907, 70, widow, Lecarrow (John Hunt, son)

Child Hunt, June 1909, 1 hour, Lecarrow (John Hunt, father)

Margaret Hunt, June 1909, 39, Lecarrow (John Hunt, husband)

John Hunt, June 1909, 70, married, Derryfad (Patrick Hunt, son)

John Hunt, May 1910, 64, married, Larganboy (Mary Johnston, daughter)

Elizabeth Hunt, Sept. 1910, 2, Drumnaderry (James Hunt, father)

Margaret Hunt, Sept. 1910, 3, Lecarrow (John Hunt)

David Hunt, Jan. 1911, 70, married, Erriff (John Hunt, son)

Norah Hunt, Feb. 1911, 77, widow, Bracklaghboy (Bridget Ryan, daughter)

Mark Hunt, May 1911, 68, Moneymore (Bridget Hunt, wife)

Thomas Hunt, July 1911, 59, married, Lecarrow (John Hunt, son)

Margaret Hunt, Nov. 1911, 90, widow, Island (Mary Hunt, daughter-in-law)

Mary Ellen Hunt, Nov, 1911, 3, Gorteen (Michael Murphy, grandfather)

Michael Hunt, Feb. 1912, 82, married, Bekan (Thomas Hunt, son)

Mary Hunt, Augt. 1912, 61, widow, Addergoole (Martin Hunt, son)

Mary Hunt, Feb. 1913, 21, Reask (James Hunt, brother)

Mary Hunt, May 1913, 86, widow, Scregg (Elizabeth ? Hunt, daughter)

John Hunt, Apr. 1914, 75, widower, Skeaghard (Michael Henry ?, son-in-law)

William Hunt, Nov. 1914, 84, married, Derrynacong (Thomas M. Hunt, son)

Mary Hunt, May 1915, 82, widow, Bekan (John Hunt)

Mary Hunt, Feb. 1917, 65, widow, Derryfad (John Hunt, son)

Bridget Hunt, Feb. 1917, 78, Mt. Delvin (Thomas Hunt, husband)

Bridget Hunt, Sept. 1917, 91, widow, Milltown (Patrick Hunt, son)

John Hunt, Nov. 1918, 93, married, Reask (James Hunt, son)

James Hunt, Nov. 1918, 18, of influenza, Scregg (Thomas Hunt, father)

Thomas M. Hunt, Nov. 1918, 32, single, of influenza, Derrynacong (Patrick Lyons)

Thomas Hunt, Jan. 1919, 3, of influenza, Moneymore (Bridget Hunt, mother)

Ellen Hunt, Jan. 1919, 80, widow, Knock Parish (Castlerea Hospital)

Catherine Hunt, March 1919, 72, widow, Brackloon (Thomas Hunt, son)

Michael Hunt, Jan. 1920, 67, married, Gorteen (James Hunt, son)

Katherine Hunt, Feb. 1921, 67, widow, Reask (John Hunt, son)

Honora Hunt, Augt 1922, 72, widow, Lecarrow (John Hunt, son)

Mary Hunt, Sept. 1922, 63, Coolnafarna (William Hunt, husband)

Mary Hunt, Nov. 1922, 64, widow, Island (Thomas Hunt, son)

Helen Mary Hunt, July 1923, 9 weeks, Derryfad (Ellen Hunt, mother)

Bridget Hunt, Dec. 1923, 80, widow, Cloonbook (Nellie Hunt, daughter-in-law)

Bridget Hunt, Apr. 1924, 74, widow, Moneymore (Michael Hunt, son)

Bridget Hunt, Augt. 1924, 62, married, Drum (James Hunt, son)

Katie Hunt, Feb. 1925, 30, married, Wingfield (Mary Kate Heneghan)

Patrick Hunt, Sept. 1925, 35, Clooncrim (Norah Hunt, wife)

James Hunt, Feb. 1926, 74, single, Bracklaghboy (Patrick Waldron, nephew)

Mary Hunt, July 1927, 71, widow, Gorteen (John Hunt, son)

Patrick Hunt, Jan. 1931, 80, married, Clooncrim (John Rush, son-in-law)

Mary Hunt, Sept. 1931, 79, widow, Clooncrim (John Rush, son-in-law)

Patrick Hunt, Feb. 1932, 86, married, Bracklagh (Nellie Hunt, daughter)

Thomas Hunt, March 1932, 93, widower, Mt. Delvin (Kathleen Costello, granddaughter)

Thomas Hunt, Apr. 1932, 70, married, Scregg (Ellie Hunt, daughter)

Michael Hunt, May 1932, 57, Erriff (Sarah Hunt, wife)

John Hunt, June 1932, 75, married, Lecarrow (Thomas Kelly, nephew)

Bridget Hunt, Nov. 1932, 72, married, Knockanarra (Mary Godfrey, daughter)

Thomas Hunt, July 1934, 51, Island (Delia Hunt, wife)

Mary Hunt, March 1935, 74, married, Derrynacong (Michael Hunt, son)

Thomas Hunt, July 1936, 55, married, Tullaghaun (James Hunt, son)

Bridget Hunt, Nov. 1936, 80, widow, Erriff (Sarah Hunt, daughter)

John Hunt, Augt. 1937, 86, widower, Pollanalty (Michael Hunt, son)

Michael Hunt, Nov. 1937, 50, married, Moneymore (Philip Hunt, son)

John Hunt, Dec. 1937, 80, widower, Killunaugher (William Brown, brother-in-law)

Mary Hunt, Sept. 1938, 81, widow, Ballyhaunis (Birdie Johnson, granddaughter)

Patrick Hunt, Dec. 1938, 77, widower, Knockanarra (Patrick Godfrey, son-in-law)

John Hunt, Apr. 1939, 70, married, Ballyhaunis (Nellie Cunningham, neighbor)

Thomas Hunt, Oct. 1939, 8 months, Derrynacong (Elizabeth Hunt, mother)

Thomas Hunt, Nov. 1939, 63, married, Brackloon (Martin O'Donnell, brother-in-law)

Mary Hunt, Dec. 1940, 71, widow, Scregg (Thomas Hunt, son)

1901 Census ~ Annagh Civil Parish ~ Heads of Household Alphabetized by Townland

Derrynacong	~ Thomas Hunt, 49, & Mary Hunt, 45
Derrynacong	~ Thomas Hunt, 30, & Anne Hunt, 25
	Bridget Boland, 62, widow
Derrynacong	~ William Hunt, 65, & Mary Hunt, 60
Knockanarra	~ Patrick Hunt, 35, & Bridget Hunt, 35
Lecarrow	~ James Hunt, 19, Anne Hunt, 17,
	Margaret Hunt, 15, John Hunt, 14 (siblings)
Lecarrow	~ John Hunt, 40, & Elizabeth Hunt, 31
	Celia Hunt, 90, widow
Lecarrow	~ John Hunt, 45, & Margaret Hunt, 31
	Bridget Hunt, 65, widow
Lecarrow	~ Thomas Hunt, 58, & Oney Hunt, 54
Lugboy Demesne	~ Bridget Hunt, 38, married
	Annie Josephine Hunt, 7, daughter
Moneymore	~ Mark Hunt, 56, & Bridget Hunt, 46
Scregg	~ Thomas Hunt, 36, & Mary A. Hunt, 30
	Mary Hunt, 60, widow
Tullaghaun	~ Patrick Kelly, 74, & Mary Kelly, 72
	Thomas Hunt, 28 & Norah Hunt, 29

1901 Census ~ Bekan Civil Parish ~ Heads of Household Alphabetized by Townland

Bracklaghboy	~ James Hunt, 45, single
Bracklaghboy	~ Michael Ryan, 45, Bridget Ryan, 40
	Honoria Hunt, 65, widow
Carrowreagh	~ Michael Hunt, 70, & Mary Hunt, 60
Cloonbookoughter	~ Bridget Hunt, 65, widow
Cloonbulban	~ Patrick Hunt, 55, & Mary Hunt, 48
	Sarah Connolly, 75, widower
Cuiltycreaghan	~ Darby Hunt, 66, & Anne Hunt, 64
Cuiltycreaghan	~ Thomas Hunt, 60, & Mary Hunt, 62
	John Hunt, 26, & Ellen Hunt, 25
Erriff	~ David Hunt, 38, & Bridget Hunt, 32
Island	~ Mary Hunt, 39, widow, & Margaret Hunt, 80, widow
Keebagh	~ Bridget Hunt, 50, widow
Keebagh	~ Thomas Hunt, 56, & Kate Hunt, 50
Killknock	~ Thomas Hunt, 31, & Mary Hunt, 30
	Nora Hunt, 64, widow
Larganboy East	~ John Hunt, 60, & Mary Hunt, 50
Reask	~ John Hunt, 74, & Catherine Hunt, 54
Skeaghard	~ John Hunt, 55, widower

1901 Census ~ Kiltullagh Civil Parish ~ Heads of Household Alphabetized by Townland

Clooncrim	~ Patrick Hunt, 50, & Mary Hunt, 40
Gorteen	~ Michael Hunt, 56, & Mary Hunt, 45
Laughil	~ Patrick Hunt, 40, & Bridget Hunt, 40
	Bridget Hunt, 75, widow
Mt. Delvin	~ Thomas Hunt, 60, & Bridget Hunt, 60
Pollanalty East	~ John Hunt, 40, & Delia Hunt, 33
	Bridget Hunt, 80, widow

Boston Pilot's "Missing Friends" column

Thomas Hunt – November 1852
Native of Derrynacull, near Ballyhavnis (Co. Mayo), who came to America in 1847—he lived two years at Reading, PA—supposed now to be in Lancaster County, PA.

Patrick Hunt – January 1883
Left Ballyhaunis, Co. Mayo, in the year 1841. When last heard he was residing in Boston (Roxbury District), Mass. Information of him will be received by his brother, Michael Hunt, 23 Grafton St., Dublin, who would be glad to hear from him or his children.

Petty Court Record

6 March 1897
John Hunt, Kiltobar, Kiltullagh, complainant
Patrick Hunt, Kiltobar, Kiltullagh, defendant

John was assaulted "under circumstance denoting a derangement of mind." Patrick was committed to Ballinasloe Lunatic asylum.

Sligo Prison Record

Thomas Hunt
1892
Charge – assault
Born Ballyhaunis, 1842
50, 5'9, dark hair, brown eyes, sallow complexion
Pock marked, teeth missing
Last residence – Rochdale ?

Calendar of Wills

Patrick Hunt of Larganboy
died 3 Dec. 1872
beneficiary – Patrick Hunt, son
effects – under 200 pounds

Patrick Hunt of Lecarrow
died 4 March 1888
beneficiary – Patrick Hunt, son
effects – under 60 pounds

Anne Hunt of Lecarrow
died 12 June 1900
beneficiary – James Hunt
effects – 18 pounds, 16 shillings

Patrick Hunt of Killunaugher
died 26 Augt. 1901
beneficiary – Bridget Grogan, wife of John Grogan
effects – 121 pounds, 17 shillings

John Hunt of Larganboy
died 7 May 1910
beneficiary – Mary Hunt, spouse
effects – 99 pounds, 10 shillings

David Hunt of Erriff
died 12 Dec. 1910
beneficiary – Michael Hunt
effects – 53 pounds, 10 shillings

William Hunt of Derrynacong
died 3 Nov. 1914
beneficiaries – John W. Hunt, Thomas Hunt
effects - 595 pounds, 7 shillings

Thomas Hunt of Mannin, Aghamore
died 17 June 1915
beneficiary – Catherine Hunt, spouse
effects – 177 pounds, 10 shillings

Fitzmaurice

The Fitzmaurice families in the vicinity of Ballyhaunis are believed to be descendants of Maurice de Prendergast, an Anglo-Norman knight who accompanied Richard de Clare (Strongbow) in the 1169 Norman invasion of Ireland. Maurice was born in 1145 in the hamlet of Prendergast in the borough of Haverfordshire in Pembrokeshire, Wales. He married Nest (Nesta) Fitzgerald of Windsor (b. 1152). They had two known children, Philip and Gerard. Maurice died near Dublin in 1205.

Originally, the Normans were Vikings who settled in Normandy, France, in the tenth century. The surname Prendergast derives from an unknown place in Flanders (possibly Brontegeest). Maurice was descended from a knight named Prenliregast who participated in William the Conquerer's 1066 invasion of England. This person's son, Philip, received land in Pembrokeshire.

Specifically, the Fitzmaurices in the vicinity of Ballyhaunis are descended from Gerard (1187 – 1251), Maurice's youngest son. Gerard would have taken the name Gerard McMaurice or, in the Irish version, Gerald Fitzmaurice. The name was sometimes written in the records as it was pronounced—Fitzmorris.

<u>Viscount Dillon's Lease Books</u>

Thomas Fitzmaurice – Addergoole, Aghamore 1788

John Fitzmaurice – Lisbaun, Bekan, 1800

Rd. Fitzmaurice – Gorteen More, Bekan 1800

Diocese of Tuam Marriage Records

Honor Fitzmaurice & Stephen Hosty
m. Nov. 1821 (Walter Fitzmaurice & Luke Hosty), Annagh Parish

John Fitzmaurice & Catherine Waldron
m. Dec. 1822 (John Fitzmaurice & Patrick Fitzmaurice), Kiltullagh Parish

Mary Fitzmaurice & Patrick Gunning
m. July 1823 (John Fitzmaurice & Catherine Waldron), Bekan Parish

Bridget Fitzmaurice & Patrick Lyons
m. Feb. 1824 (Michael Moon ? & John Lyons), Annagh

Mary Fitzmaurice & John Gormelly
m. Feb. 1824 (Thomas Fitzmaurice & Patrick Fitzmaurice), Bekan

Mary Fitzmaurice & Thomas Johnson
m. Apr. 1824 (John Fitzmaurice & Patrick Johnson), Annagh

Martin Fitzmaurice & Catherine Kelly
m. May 1824 (Michael Fitzmaurice & John ?), Annagh

Peter Fitzmaurice & Mary Freely
m. Oct. 1825 (Michael Fitzmaurice & Mary Freely), Bekan

Mary Fitzmaurice & Thomas Friely
m. Oct. 1825 (Luke Friely & Lau Murphy), Annagh

William Fitzmaurice & Catherine Hoban
m. Jan. 1826 (Thomas McNamarrow & Margaret Nolean), Bekan

Bridget Fitzmaurice & Dermot Loftis
m. Feb. 1826 (Patrick Fitzmaurice & Martin Fitzmaurice), Annagh

Catherine Fitzmaurice & James Jordan
m. Feb. 1826 (Michael Fitzmaurice & Anne Fitzmaurice), Bekan

Nelly Fitzmaurice & Thomas Green
m. Feb. 1826 (Patrick Fitzmaurice & Timothy Fitzmaurice), Bekan

Mary Fitzmaurice & Timothy Raftery
m. Feb. 1827 (Thomas Fitzmaurice & William Nolan), Annagh

Tithe Applotment Books, 1833

Patrick Fitzmaurice - Half the Wood (Lecarrow), Annagh Parish

Michael Fitzmaurice - Grallagh, Bekan Parish

Michael Fitzmaurice - Togher, Bekan

Patrick Fitzmaurice - Forthill, Bekan

Patrick Fitzmaurice - Kilmannin, Bekan

Patrick Fitzmaurice - Mountain, Bekan

Unnamed Fitzmaurice - Tawnaghmore, Bekan

Patrick Fitzmaurice - Little Castlequarter, Kiltullagh Parish

House Book - Feb. 1855

Myles Fitzmaurice, Abbeyquarter, Annagh Parish (Patrick Forde, lessor)

Patrick Fitzmaurice, Hazelhill, Annagh Parish (Walter Burke, lessor)

Griffith's Valuation – 1856

Bridget Fitzmaurice - Barheen, Annagh Parish

Catherine Fitzmaurice - Barheen

Dennis Ford

John Fitzmaurice - Derrynacong

John Fitzmaurice - Gorteen

John Fitzmaurice - Tonregee

Patrick Fitzmaurice - Ballyhaunis

Patrick Fitzmaurice - Barheen

Patrick Fitzmaurice - Derrynacong

Patrick Fitzmaurice (widow) - Derrynacong

Patrick Fitzmaurice - Woodpark

Peter Fitzmaurice - Barheen

Thomas Fitzmaurice - Pattenspark

David Fitzmaurice - Brackloon North, Bekan Parish

David Fitzmaurice - Mountain

Honoria Fitzmaurice - Togher

James Fitzmaurice - Bekan

John Fitzmaurice - Brackloon North

John Fitzmaurice - Forthill

John Fitzmaurice - Kilmannin

John Fitzmaurice - Reask

Mark Fitzmaurice - Forthill

Mary Fitzmaurice - Mountain

Mary Fitzmaurice - Reask

Michael Fitzmaurice - Brackloon South

Patrick Fitzmaurice - Reask

Patrick Fitzmaurice - Tawnaghmore

Patrick Fitzmaurice - Togher

Peter Fitzmaurice - Forthill

Peter Fitzmaurice - Larganboy West

Thomas Fitzmaurice - Brackloon North

Thomas Fitzmaurice - Lisbaun East

Thomas Fitzmaurice - Mountain

William Fitzmaurice - Lisbaun East

Martin Fitzmaurice - Clydagh Lower, Kiltullagh Parish

Patrick Fitzmaurice - Castlequarter

Peter Fitzmaurice - Clooncalgy Beg

Peter Fitzmaurice - Cloonlee

Annagh, Bekan & Kiltullagh Parish
Registers, Baptisms and Marriages

Bridget Fitzmaurice & Thomas Sloyan / Sloyne
Mary, Sept. 1832 (John Sloyne & Sara Fitzmaurice), Brackloon North

Eleanor, June 1833 (Denis Sloyne & Nelly Narry)
Catherine, July 1834 (Peter Fitzmaurice & Mary Moore)
Winifred, March 1837 (Henry ? & Nelly ?) [record requires verification]
John, March 1840 (Patrick Narry & Bridget Flatley)
Thomas, Nov. 1842 (John Fitzmaurice & Mary Sloyne) [date requires verification]
James, July 1845 (Martin Flatley & Bridget Flatley)
Mary, March 1849 (John Fitzmaurice & Mary Shean)

Note: Bridget's name was also given as Mary.

Thomas Fitzmaurice & Mary Fitzmaurice
Judy, Sept. 1832 (no sponsors), Bekan
Catherine, 1835 (John Fitzmaurice & ? Fitzmaurice) [date requires verification]
Catherine, 1836 (? Johnson & ??) [date requires verification]
Mary, Oct. 1837 (John Murphy & Catherine Dyer)
Andrew, Sept. 1845 (Thomas Hoban & Honor Dyer)
Honor, Nov. 1846 (James Moran & Judith Fitzmaurice)

Patrick Fitzmaurice & Mary Murray
Catherine, Nov. 1832 (Austin Murray & Mary Curley), Bekan [date requires verification]

James Fitzmaurice & Mary Grogan
Mary, Nov. 1833 (Patrick Fitzmaurice & Cecily Henry), Bekan

Celia Fitzmaurice & Edward (or William) Finn
Thomas, Dec. 1833 (John Finn & Mary Finn), Bekan
Anne, Feb. 1847 (John Fitzmaurice & Bridget Fitzmaurice)

Ellen Fitzmaurice & Patrick Shean
James, July 1834 (Anthony Waldron & Bridget Waldron), Bekan
Henry, Sept. 1836 (James Waldron & Rose Morrelly)

Mary Fitzmaurice & Thomas Shean
Catherine, July 1834 (Peter Fitzmaurice & Mary Moore), Bekan

Winifred, March 1837 (Henry Shean & ? Shean)
Mary, June 1843 (Patrick Morrally & Catherine Fitzmaurice)
Margaret, March 1849 (John Fitzmaurice & Mary Shean)

Martin Fitzmaurice & Honoria Fitzmaurice
Sarah, Augt. 1834 (Michael Fitzmaurice & ? Fitzmaurice), Togher
David, Nov. 1836 (Michael Fitzmaurice & Cecily Fitzmaurice)

Mark Fitzmaurice & Bridget Hunt
Thomas, Sept. 1834 (Philip Hunt & Mary Hunt), Bekan
John, 1836 (? Carroll & Mary Anne Carroll)
Mary Oct. 1837 (Patrick Fitzmaurice & Catherine Sloyan)
John, Apr. 1846 (Edward Hunt & Sara Hunt)

William Fitzmaurice & Catherine Hoban
Mary, Feb. 1835 (Michael Fitzmaurice & Honor Cox), Leo

Note: see the Tuam marriage register for this couple.

Bridget Fitzmaurice & Thomas Grogan
m. March 1835 (? Henry & Catherine Fitzmaurice), Bekan [date requires verification]

Bridget Fitzmaurice & Thomas Infant
m. March 1835 (Henry M- & Catherine Fitzmaurice), Bekan

Mary Fitzmaurice & John Gormandy
Mary, Apr. 1835 (Michael Fitzmaurice & Catherine Fitzmaurice), Bekan
Patrick Oct. 1837 (John Smyth & Mary Griffin)

Note: this may be the same couple listed in the Tuam Marriage Register as Mary Fitzmaurice & John Gormelly.

Thomas Fitzmaurice & ? Hunt
Hannah ?, June 1835 (sponsors illegible), Bekan [name requires verification]

Mary Fitzmaurice & Myles Waldron
m. Jan. 1836 (Patrick Waldron & Mary Dyer) Bekan
Mary, Jan. 1838 (Patrick Higgins & Mary Dyer)

Thomas Fitzmaurice & Mary Caulfield
John, May 1836 (Michael Fitzmaurice & Mary Fitzmaurice), Bekan
Ellen, Sept. 1838 (Michael Fitzmaurice & ? Keane)
David, Sept. 1845 (David Fitzmaurice & Catherine Flatley)

John Fitzmaurice & Honor Keane
m. 1836 (John Keane & Mary Keane), Bekan [date requires verification]
Mary, July 1840 (Michael McDonough & Sara Keane), Tonregee

Note: in the marriage record the name was given as Margaret Keane.

Ellen Fitzmaurice & Michael Flatley
Anne, 1836 (sponsors illegible), Bekan [record requires verification]
Bridget, 1838 (Patrick Fitzmaurice & Bridget Fitzmaurice) [date requires verification]

Note: see the record below for Ellen Fitzmaurice & Patrick Flatley.

Thomas Fitzmaurice & Honor Flatley
m. Feb. 1837 (Richard Fitzmaurice & Catherine Flatley), Bekan [requires verification]
John, June 1838 (William Fitzmaurice & Bridget Waldron)
Richard, June 1838 twin (Patrick Flatley & Bridget Flatley)
David, March 1843 (John Fitzmaurice & W. Ryan ?)
John, Jan. 1846 (Thomas Flatley & Mary Flatley)
John, Feb. 1848 (Thomas Hopkins & Ellen Fitzmaurice)

Mary Fitzmaurice & Thomas Greally
m. Feb. 1837 (James Culliney & Mary Hunt), Bekan [year needs verification]
Catherine, Apr. 1838 (Michael Greally & Eleanor Greally)
Mary, Apr. 1846 (James Grogan & Bridget Flatley)
Mary, May 1850 (Michael Nowlan & Cecilia Fitzmaurice)
Thomas, Apr. 1857 (John Waldron & Bridget Hessian)

John Fitzmaurice & Bridget Kearn
m. Feb. 1837 (John Kearn & Mary Kearn), Bekan

Michael Fitzmaurice & Mary Smyth
m. Feb. 1837 (John Fitzmaurice & Mary McGarry), Bekan

Mary Fitzmaurice & John Kelly [name requires verification]
Patrick, March 1837 (Pat Hill ?, Pat Kissane, Mary Keane & Peggy Keane)
Bridget, July 1843 (Michael Cunnane & Ellen R-), Bekan [date requires verification]
Bernard, March 1845 (John Mangan ? & Mary Egan)

Note: the date for Patrick's baptism requires verification. The register listed four sponsors.

John Fitzmaurice & Catherine Waldron
John, May 1837 (Timothy ? & Cecily Fitzmaurice), Bekan
Ellen, June 1848 (John Fitzmaurice & Cecily Fitzmaurice)

Note: see the Tuam Marriage Register for a couple with the same name.

James Fitzmaurice & Bridget Grogan
Martin, Oct. 1837 (Henry Lyons & Peggy Grogan), Bekan
James, Sept. 1844 (Patrick Cunnane & Mary Grogan)

David Fitzmaurice & Bridget Dyer
m. Feb. 1838 (Patrick Barrett & Ellen Fitzmaurice), Bekan
Catherine, Augt. 1852 (Patrick Waldron & Catherine Hoban)
Thomas, March 1856 (Patrick Fitzmaurice & Mary Barrett)

Mary Fitzmaurice & Thomas Johnson
James, March 1838 (Thomas Morrily & Mary Haddican), Bekan

Note: see the Tuam marriage register for a couple with the same name.

Sarah Fitzmaurice & William Devaney
m. July 1838 (David Fitzmaurice & Ellen Fitzmaurice), Bekan

Catherine Fitzmaurice & Martin Regan
m. Sept. 1838 (Peter Regan & Cecily Fitzmaurice)
Ellen, Nov. 1841 (Thomas Regan & Mary Foley), Bakillian ?, Kiltullagh
Michael, Augt. 1845 (William Regan & B-)

John Fitzmaurice & Anne Fitzmaurice
John, Sept. 1838 (Thomas Fitzmaurice & Cecily Fitzmaurice), Bekan

Note: couple with same names in 1861 below.

Martin Fitzmaurice & Margaret Rogers
Margaret, Feb. 1840 (Patrick Rogers & Mary Fitzmaurice), Clydagh
Honor, May 1842 (Michael O'Brien & Mary Fitzmaurice)
Ellen, June 1844 (Peter Lyons & Catherine Cole)
Martin, Oct. 1846 (Austin Fitzmaurice & Mary Lyons)
Austin, June 1850 (Thomas Waldron)

Catherine Fitzmaurice & Hugh Murphy
m. March 1840 (Thomas Waldron & Honor Murphy), Kiltullagh
James, Feb. 1841 (Thomas Fitzgerald & Ellen Fitzmaurice), Rabbit
Burrow, Kiltullagh
Mary, Oct. 1843 (Thomas McLoughlin & Bridget Fitzmaurice)
Bridget, ? 1845 [record needs to be verified]
Patrick, Apr. 1850 (Michael Fitzmaurice)
Bridget, Dec. 1852 (Margaret Gibbons & James Gibbons)
Catherine, Sept. 1855 (Thomas Egan & Mary Murphy)
Margaret, Jan. 1858 (? O'Brien & Kate Waldron)
Ellen, Augt. 1863 (Patrick Keane & Honor Collins)

Note: Catherine was from Laughil. Hugh was from Rabbit Burrow.
Catherine Murphy, widow, died Augt. 1899, age given as 82. Catherine
Duffy, daughter, was the informant.

Honor Fitzmaurice & John Henaghan
Patrick, July 1840 (Margaret Fitzmaurice), Grange, Kiltullagh
John, Feb. 1843 (Dermot Loftus & Bridget Fitzmaurice)
Martin, Feb. 1846 (Catherine Connor)

Note: this may be the same family listed below in May 1844.

Patrick Fitzmaurice & Catherine McHugh
Bridget, July 1840 (Thomas Flynn & Bridget Keane), Castlequarter
David, Dec. 1842 (Peter Hevron & Anne Keane)
Catherine, July 1845 (Mary Hevron)
Patrick, Jan. 1848 (Thomas Hefferaw ? & Mary Neenan ?)

Ellen Fitzmaurice & Thomas Green
Michael, Jan. 1841 (Bryan Green & Catherine McDermott), Clooncalgy

Note: see Tuam marriage record for a couple with this name.

Margaret Fitzmaurice & Michael Harte
m. Feb. 1841 (Thomas Harte & Mary Henaghen), Kiltullagh

Note: Margaret was from Laughil. Michael was from Bekan Parish.

Bridget Fitzmaurice & Michael Flynn
John, June 1841 (John Flynn & Winifred Harkin), Clooncrim
Michael, Oct. 1843 (Thomas Lawless & Catherine Lawless)
Patrick, Oct. 1846 (Mary Flynn) [date requires verification]
Patrick, Oct. 1849 (John Flynn & Mary Kane)
Andrew, Augt. 1857 (John Caulfield & Honoria Gormelly ?)

Mary Fitzmaurice & Peter Lyons
Patrick, May 1842 (Austin Fitzmaurice & Mary Rogers) [name requires verification]
Michael, July 1844 (Bridget Fitzmaurice), Clydagh
Michael, June 1845 (Michael Lyons & Mary Rogers)
John, Apr. 1848 (John Fitzmaurice & Mary Hussey) [date requires verification]]
Patrick, March 1852 (John Fitzmaurice & Margaret Reilly)
Martin, Sept. 1854 (James Lyons & Bridget Fitzmaurice)
Honoria, Apr. 1857 (Margaret Fitzmaurice & Michael Lyons)
Peter, Augt. 1859 (Michael Casserly & Margaret Fitzmaurice)

Bridget Fitzmaurice & Thomas Keane
John, Jan. 1843 (Patrick Keane & Mary Flatley), Bekan
Michael, March 1845 (Michael Lyons & Ellen Fitzmaurice)
Mary, Jan. 1847 (Michael Lyons & Bridget Keane)
Patrick, June 1851 (James H- & Catherine Egan)

Note: in Patrick's record the mother's name was given as Mary.

Myles Fitzmaurice & Bridget Grogan
Patrick, June 1843 (James Fitzmaurice & Peggy Fitzmaurice), Bekan
Margaret, July 1846 (David Lyons & Mary ?)
Bridget, July 1848 (Michael Grogan & Mary Murphy)
James, Oct. 1850 (Thady Duffy & Mary Duffy)

Margaret Fitzmaurice & James Duggan
Martin, Jan. 1844 (Bernard Duggan & Mary Riley ?), Bekan
Anne, Augt. 1846 (Martin Duggan & Mary Mulloy) [record requires verification]
Bridget, Apr. 1849 (Martin Finn & Catherine Cunnane)
William, Augt. 1853 (Patrick Fitzmaurice & Mary Haddican)
Margaret, Sept. 1859 (Edmund Molloy & Bridget Kelly)

Patrick Fitzmaurice & Nancy Kyne (Coyne)
m. March 1844 (Thomas Fitzmaurice & Nancy Burke), Bekan
John, Feb. 1845 (Michael Kyne & Bridget Keane ?)

Note: in John's record the mother's name was given as Anne.

Honor Fitzmaurice & John Henaghan
John, May 1844 (Bridget Raftery), Tonraree
Anne, July 1846 (Mary O'Brien)

Mary Fitzmaurice & Martin Moran
m. July 1844 (Patrick Moran & Bridget Grogan) [date requires verification]
Mary, July 1844 ? (Patrick Moran & Bridget Grogan), Togher [date requires verification]
Mary, Sept. 1845 (Patrick Fitzmaurice & Bridget Fitzmaurice)

David Fitzmaurice & Mary Brennan
Mary, Sept. 1844 (Patrick Brennan & Martin Wade ?)

Ellen Fitzmaurice & Patrick Flatley
Martin, Oct. 1844 (Thomas Nolan & Bridget Waldron), Bekan

Honor Fitzmaurice & James Hunt
m. Jan. 1845 (Michael Hunt & Honor Flatley), Bekan
Ellen, Nov. 1854 (Thomas Fitzmaurice & Biddy Morley), Annagh
Child, Oct. 1858 (Mary Waldron & John Fitzmaurice)
Child, ?? 1862 (? & Thomas Fitzmaurice) [record requires verification]

Anne Fitzmaurice & Bryan Connel ? [name requires verification]
Bridget, March 1845 (? Connor & Mary Connel), Bekan

Note: see the record below for Nancy Fitzmaurice & Bryan Connell.

Catherine Fitzmaurice & Bernard Graham
Catherine, Apr. 1845 (Patrick Fitzmaurice & ? Leeson), Bekan
Bernard, Nov. 1846 (Michael Fitzmaurice & Kate Griffin)
Catherine, June 1848 (Patrick Graham & Bridget Leeson)

William Fitzmaurice & Kate Flatley
Kate, June 1845 (Patrick McNamara & Jane Flatley), Bekan

Bartly Fitzmaurice & Ellen Frehilly
m. July 1845 (Michael Boland & Ellen Brennan), Bekan

Mary Fitzmaurice & Thomas Hefron
James, July 1845 (Martin Flatley & Bridget Flatley), Bekan

John Fitzmaurice & ? Fitzmaurice
Anne, Sept. 1845 (Michael Fitzmaurice & Celia Fitzmaurice), Bekan

James Fitzmaurice & Mary Fitzmaurice
Anne, Oct. 1845 (Henry Fitzmaurice & Bridget Hunt), Bekan
Martin, Feb. 1847 (Martin Fitzmaurice & ? Hunt)

Mary Fitzmaurice & Thomas Hican [name requires verification]
Ellen, Nov. 1845 (Martin Finn & Sara Finn), Bekan

John Fitzmaurice & Bridget Waldron
Andrew, Nov. 1845 (Patrick Waldron & Mary Devany), Bekan

Mary Fitzmaurice & Thomas Moran [name requires verification]
Ellen, Nov. 1845 (Martin Finn & Sarah Finn), Bekan

Patrick Fitzmaurice & Bridget Mulclear [name requires verification]
Kate, Feb. 1846 (Thomas Fahy & Mary Fahy), Bekan

David Fitzmaurice & Anne McNamara
James, Feb. 1846 (James McNamara), Bekan [date requires verification]
John, June 1848 (Patrick McNamara & Bridget McNamara), Bekan
Thomas, Augt. 1851 (Thomas Hoban & Bridget Hoban)
Margaret, Jan. 1856 (John Flatley & Margaret Hoban)

Note: in Thomas's record the mother's name was given as Nancy.

Michael Fitzmaurice & Honor Noone
Patrick, March 1846 (John Fitzmaurice & Mary Fitzmaurice), Bekan

Patrick Fitzmaurice & Mary Waldron
m. March 1846 (John Fitzmaurice & Mary Waldron) Bekan
Mary, Nov. 1852 (John Kelly & Mary Waldron), Derrynacong
Margaret, Apr. 1855 [record needs to be verified]
Judith, Nov. 1856 (Michael Connell & Mary Fitzmaurice)
Mary, 1857 (Michael Fitzmaurice & ?) [record needs to be verified]
Bridget, Feb. 1859 (Patrick & ? & ? Bones)
Patrick, Feb. 1866 (civil record)
Honoria, Nov. 1868 (civil record)

Patrick Fitzmaurice & Catherine Fitzmaurice
Patrick, June 1846 (Thomas Heffernan & Mary Neenan), Pollanalty

Thady Fitzmaurice & Honor Groake
Catherine, July 1846 (Patrick Fitzmaurice & Catherine Groake), Bekan

Patrick Fitzmaurice & Bridget Kilkenny
Michael, Dec. 1846 (Edmund Kilkenny & Mary Fitzmaurice), Bekan
Timothy, March 1849 (Michael Fitzmaurice & Sara Fitzmaurice)
Edmund, June 1851 (Patrick Kilkenny & Cecilia Fitzmaurice)
Ellen, Nov. 1855 (Timothy Fitzmaurice & Catherine Fitzmaurice)

Note: Bridget was from Uro ? in Kiltullagh Parish. Her name was given
as Ellinore in Ellen's record.

Peter Fitzmaurice & Bridget Frehilly
Margaret, Jan. 1847 (Thomas Fitzmaurice & Kate Fitzmaurice), Bekan

Myles Fitzmaurice & Bridget Kelly
m. Jan. 1847 (Michael Fitzmaurice & Mary Fitzmaurice), Bekan
Patrick, July 1843 (Patrick Fitzmaurice & Bridget Madden)
Thomas, Nov. 1844 (Michael Fitzmaurice & Honor Noone)
Myles, Jan. 1847 (Patrick Fitzmaurice & Ann Kelly)
Andrew, Nov. 1849 (Owen Nolan & Catherine Nolan)
James, Augt. 1852 (? Hunt & ??)
John, March 1855 (Patrick Fitzmaurice & Bedelia Stuart ?)

Note: they were married in Kiltullagh Parish. Date of marriage needs to
be verified.

Patrick Fitzmaurice & Mary Fitzmaurice
Martin, Feb. 1847 (Martin Fitzmaurice & ? Hunt), Bekan
Martin, Feb. 1855 (Thomas Finnegan & Mary Finnegan), Annagh

Bridget Fitzmaurice & Michael Bailey
m. March 1847 (Thomas Cribbin & Bridget Cox), Kiltullagh

Mary Fitzmaurice & John Murphy
Michael, Oct. 1847 (Myles Fitzmaurice & Mary Fitzmaurice), Bekan
Bridget, Feb. 1850 (Patrick Devany & Bridget Fitzmaurice)
Patrick, Augt. 1859 (Edward Tarpey & Ellen Fitzmaurice)

Ellen Fitzmaurice & Patrick Diskin
m. Oct. 1847 (John King & Bridget Fitzmaurice), Kiltullagh
Catherine, Nov. 1848 (? Fitzmaurice & Bridget Fitzmaurice), Corrasluastia
Mary, March 1850 (Patrick D- & Anne Finnegan)
Bridget, June 1853 (Bridget Fitzmaurice & John Diskin)
Margaret, Jan. 1855 (Patrick Fitzmaurice & Mary ?)
Thomas, Dec. 1856 (Patrick Fitzmaurice & Bridget Fitzmaurice)
Patrick, May 1859 (Patrick Frehilly & Mary Frehilly)

John Fitzmaurice & Betty Kyne [name requires verification]
Bridget, Jan. 1848 (Thomas Waldron & Bridget Waldron), Bekan

Martin Fitzmaurice & Bridget Hunt
Patrick, June 1848 (John Keadon & Mary Keadon), Bekan

Mary Fitzmaurice & Thomas Lyons
Kate, Dec. 1848 (Peter Devine & Bridget Lyons), Bekan

Honor Fitzmaurice & Dominick Higgins
Kate, Dec. 1848 (Thomas Higgins & Mary Higgins)
Mary, July 1850 (Patrick Forde & Catherine Dyer), Brackloon South
Michael, Sept. 1855 (James Waldron & Mary Higgins)
Patrick, Feb. 1858 (James Waldron & Bridget Fitzmaurice)

John Fitzmaurice & Rose Caulfield
Mary, June 1849 (James Fitzmaurice & Mary P-)

Sabina Fitzmaurice & Edmund Fynn / Finn
Edmund, Jan. 1850 (Thomas Shean & Bridget Waldron), Reask

Patrick Fitzmaurice & Bridget Kyne / Coyne
m. Jan. 1850 (Martin Flatley & Ellen Burke), Bekan
Bridget, Sept. 1854 (Patrick Flatley & Bridget Flanagan), Bekan
Anne, Apr. 1860 (John Fitzmaurice & Bridget Flatley)
Aloysius ?, June 1862 (Patrick Nowlan & Anne Flatley) [name requires verification]
Patrick, Augt. 1864 (civil record), Tawnaghmore

Peter, July 1867 (Thomas Fitzmaurice & Sara Fitzmaurice)
Ellen, July 1869 (Thomas Fitzmaurice & Mary Waldron)
David, Sept. 1871 (civil record; Mary Fitzmaurice present)

Note: parish register notes that Anne married in June 1909 in America.

Peter Fitzmaurice & Bridget Hopkins
m. March 1850 (John Fitzmaurice & Catherine Hopkins), Bekan
Mary, Feb. 1851 (John Fitzmaurice & Mary Hopkins)
John, Augt. 1852 (Michael Cunnane & Mary Haddican)
Bridget, Augt. 1853 (Peter Hopkins & Ellen Walsh)

Michael Fitzmaurice & Ellen McDonnell
m. Apr. 1850 (James McDonnell & Jane McDonnell), Kiltullagh
Myles, Feb. 1851 (?? & ? Fitzmaurice), Bekan
Martin, Nov. 1855 (Mark Flatley & Catherine Fitzmaurice), Clooncrim
Mary, Dec. 1859 (John Fitzmaurice & Mary Fitzmaurice)

Nancy Fitzmaurice & Bryan Connell [name requires verification]
Eleanor, June 1850 (James Plunkett & Mary Johnston), Bekan

Patrick Fitzmaurice & Mary Higgins
Thomas, Dec. 1850 (Thomas Fitzmaurice & Bridget Hunt), Bekan
Michael, July 1855 (Patrick Fitzmaurice & Mary Higgins)
Patrick, Feb. 1858 (Peter Fitzmaurice & Mary Waldron)

Note: in Thomas's baptism record the father's name was given as Michael.
See the reference below to Patrick Fitzmaurice & Mary Higgins.

Thomas Fitzmaurice & Bridget Morally
Cecilia, Dec. 1850 (John Fitzmaurice & Honor Fitzmaurice), Bekan

Note: this may be the same family as Thomas Fitzmaurice & Bridget
Morley below.

Mark Fitzmaurice & Bridget Fitzmaurice
Mark, June 1851 (Michael Fitzmaurice & Mary Fitzmaurice), Bekan

Patrick Fitzmaurice & Ellen Morris
Michael, Nov. 1851 (Kate Morris), Barheen [location requires verification]
John, Feb. 1856 (Pt. ? & K- Fitzmaurice)

Note: see the record below for John Fitzmaurice & Ellen Morris.

Bridget Fitzmaurice & John Flatley
Mary, Nov. 1851 (Andrew Flatley & Ellen Fitzmaurice), Bekan
Bridget, Jan. 1856 (Thomas Fitzmaurice & Mary Flatley)
James, Feb. 1857 (Michael Fitzmaurice & Catherine Waldron)
Catherine, Dec. 1859 (Peter Waldron & Mary Fitzmaurice)

Patrick Fitzmaurice & Mary H-
Michael, Dec. 1851 (Kate H- & ?), Barheen

John Fitzmaurice & Bridget Moran
Mary, June 1852 (John Moran & Margaret Moran), Bekan
Bridget, Dec. 1854 (Patrick Moran & Bridget Greally)
John, May 1856 (James Moran & Mary Frehilly)
Anne, Dec. 1857 (James Fitzmaurice & Bridget Fitzmaurice)
Margaret, July 1859 (Patrick Fitzmaurice & Catherine Moran)

Thomas Fitzmaurice & Mary Grady
Mary, Augt. 1852 (James Jordan & Ellen Frehilly), Bekan

Bridget Fitzmaurice & Michael Forde
Mary, Augt. 1852 (Patrick Fitzmaurice & Anne Fitzmaurice) Bekan
Thomas, Dec. 1854 (Michael Forde & Bridget Morley)
Judith, Feb. 1860 (Anthony Forde & Bridget Finn) [name requires verification]
Bridget, Dec. 1863 (Thomas Forde & Catherine Forde)
John, June 1864 (civil record), Reask
Anne, Sept. 1867 (Michael Forde & Mary Fitzmaurice)
Andrew, Oct. 1869 (Thomas Forde & Mary Fitzmaurice)
Ellen, Sept. 1872 (Peter Fitzmaurice & Mary Lydon; Anne Veasy present)

Thomas Fitzmaurice & Bridget Morley
Mary, Nov. 1852 (Anthony Morley & Margaret Morley), Bekan
Michael, Augt. 1855 (Anthony Morley & Bridget Fitzmaurice)

Note: this may be the same family listed below as Patrick Fitzmaurice & Bridget Morley

Patrick Fitzmaurice & Mary Noon
Michael, Nov. 1852 (Kate Moran), Annagh

Mary Fitzmaurice & Patrick Connor
m. Jan. 1853 (Thomas Connor & Margaret Hevoran ?), Kiltullagh

John Fitzmaurice & Mary Waldron
David, Jan. 1853 (Michael Ryan & Bridget Nowlan), Bekan
Bridget, Nov. 1857 (James Waldron & Catherine Waldron)

Bridget Fitzmaurice & Patrick Hunt
m. Feb. 1853 (Peter Fitzmaurice & Bridget Loftus), Kiltullagh
Mary, Augt. 1854 (Patrick Flynn & Bridget Hunt), Laughil
Hugh, Jan. 1858 (James Cox & Anne Dodd)
Patrick, Nov. 1859 (Patrick Fitzmaurice & Bridget Fitzmaurice)
Michael, Oct. 1862 (Catherine Discon)
Thomas, Jan. 1870 (Timothy Flynn & Catherine Flynn)

Note: Bridget was from Laughil. Patrick was from Annagh Parish.

Mary Fitzmaurice & Patrick Grogan
James, Feb. 1853 (Mary Waldron), Derrynacong

Mary Fitzmaurice & Michael Flatley
m. Feb. 1853 (Martin Flatley & Cecilia Fitzmaurice), Bekan
Mary, Apr. 1855 (John Fitzmaurice & Honora Fitzmaurice)
Michael, March 1859 (John Fitzmaurice & Catherine Fitzmaurice)
Timothy, Nov. 1860 (John Fitzmaurice & Catherine Fitzmaurice)
Michael, Nov. 1865 (Daniel Flatley & Bridget Fitzmaurice), Forthill
Patrick, Dec. 1867 (Thomas Flatley & Sarah Flatley), Gorteen More

Patrick Fitzmaurice & Bridget Morley
Catherine, Nov. 1853 (John Fitzmaurice & Mary Morley), Bekan
Thomas, Dec. 1855 (Michael ? & Mary Haddican)
Patrick, Dec. 1857 (Martin Waldron & Anne Fitzmaurice)
Anne, July 1861 (Patrick Hopkins & Bridget Hopkins)
Honoria, June 1863 (Peter Fitzmaurice & Bridget Fitzmaurice)
Margaret, June 1865 (civil record), Reask
John, July 1867 (civil record; Mary Fitzmaurice of Reask present)
Patrick, Feb. 1870 (civil record)
Catherine, Sept. 1872 (civil record; Thomas Fitzmaurice of Larganboy present)
Ellen, Augt. 1875 (civil record), Cherryfield

Michael Fitzmaurice & Sara Flatley
m. Jan. 1854 (Martin Flatley & Bridget Flanagan), Bekan
Catherine, Dec. 1854 (Timothy Flatley & Catherine Fitzmaurice)
John, Dec. 1856 (Michael Flatley & Bridget Flatley) [date requires verification]
Michael, June 1861 (Michael Flanagan & Mary Murphy)
Timothy, June 1864 (civil record), Forthill
Mary, Jan. 1867 (civil record)
Sara, Oct. 1869 (civil record)
Sibina, Nov. 1870 (James C- & Mary Fitzmaurice) [record requires verification]
Patrick, Augt. 1873 (civil record; Catherine Fitzmaurice of Forthill present)

John Fitzmaurice & Ellen Mannion
m. Feb. 1854 (Patrick Fitzmaurice & Catherine Lyons), Bekan

John Fitzmaurice – certificate to marry outside of Annagh Parish
Feb. 1854, Derrynacong

Mary Fitzmaurice & Thomas Finnegan
m. Feb. 1854 (Hugh Lyons & Mary Sloyen), Annagh
John, Nov. 1855 (James Finnegan & Kate Fitzmaurice)

Mary Fitzmaurice & James McDonnell
m. March 1854 (Patrick Fitzmaurice & John Fitzmaurice), Annagh

Cecilia Fitzmaurice & Patrick Frehilly
m. Apr. 1854 (John Frehilly & Sabina Fitzmaurice), Bekan
Charles, Feb. 1864 (Charles Frehilly & Catherine Garrahan) [record requires verification]

Note: see reference below to Sara (Sabina) Fitzmaurice & Patrick Frehilly.

Peter Fitzmaurice & Anne Judge
m. Dec. 1854 (Peter Fitzmaurice & M-), Annagh
Mary, Nov. 1860 (Patrick Fitzmaurice & Margaret Fitzmaurice), Bekan

Note: This may be the same family listed below as Peter Fitzmaurice & Anne Brehony.

John Fitzmaurice & Bridget Fitzmaurice
Bridget, Dec. 1854 (Patrick Moran & Bridget Greally), Bekan
Catherine, Sept. 1861 (John Frehilly & Joanna Frehilly)

Mary Fitzmaurice & James Maughan
m. Jan. 1855 (Michael Fitzmaurice & Catherine Maughan), Bekan
John, Feb. 1857 (John Maughan & Catherine Maughan), Bekan

Mark Fitzmaurice & Mary Grogan
Sabina, Jan. 1855 (Michael Grogan & Maria Fitzmaurice), Bekan

John Fitzmaurice & Cecilia Fitzmaurice
Margaret, Feb. 1855 (Thomas Fre- & Sara Fitzmaurice), Bekan

Michael Fitzmaurice & Margaret Hoban
m. Feb. 1855 (John Cribbin & Margaret Hoban), Bekan
Michael, Jan. 1856 (Michael Fitzmaurice & Ellen McDonnell)

Bridget Fitzmaurice & John Connelly
m. Feb. 1855 (Edward Jordan & Mary Frehilly), Bekan

Mary, Nov. 1857 (Thomas Connelly & Bridget Connelly), Kiltullagh
Patrick, Jan. 1860 (William Connelly & Nelly Joyce)
Peter, June 1865 (Patrick Ruane & Catherine Rogers), Ballyglass

Bridget Fitzmaurice & Edward Tarpey
m. March 1855 (John Cribbin & Mary Fitzmaurice), Bekan
Thomas, Apr. 1856 (John Fitzmaurice & Catherine ?)
Mary, Oct. 1857 (Patrick Grogan & Mary Grogan)
Bridget, May 1859 (James Grogan & Bridget Morris)
Mary, Nov. 1862 (P. Tarpey & Mary Grogan)

Patrick Fitzmaurice & Ellen Fitzmaurice
Ellen, Nov. 1855 (Patrick Fitzmaurice & Honoria Stuart), Anagh

Note: Ellen's name may be Elizabeth. See references below to Patrick
Fitzmaurice & Ellen Morris and Patrick Fitzmaurice & Ellen Dyer.

Anne Fitzmaurice & Roger Vesey / Vahey / Veasy
m. Jan. 1856 (Martin Lyons & Catherine Hopkins), Bekan
Bridget, July 1857 (John Fitzmaurice & Bridget Fitzmaurice) [date requires
verification]
Mary, July 1860 (Michael Prendergast & Bridget Waldron)
Anne, Sept. 1863 (Michael Regan & Bridget Fitzmaurice)
Anne, July 1869 (civil record), Reask
John, Oct. 1871 (civil record; Bridget Vesey of Reask present)

Patrick Fitzmaurice & Mary Bride
Thomas, Jan. 1856 (Martin Bride & Margaret Bride), Derrynacong
Mary, Feb. ? 1861 (Patrick Fitzmaurice & Kate Killian) [date requires
verification]
Michael, Jan. 1865 (civil record)
Patrick, Sept. 1868 (Thomas Killian & Anne Killeen)

John Fitzmaurice & Ellen Morris [name requires verification]
John, March 1856 (Patrick Fitzmaurice & Honoria Fitzmaurice), Eden,
Annagh
Michael, 1858 (James ? Devine & Mary Morris) [date requires verification]

Ellen Fitzmaurice & Peter Dolan
[Certificate to Peter to marry outside parish, May 1855]
John, Apr. 1856 (John Fitzmaurice & Anne Connelly), Clooncalgy
Honoria, Sept. 1857 (Michael Dolan & Sara Fitzmaurice)
Patrick, Nov. 1859 (Catherine Fitzmaurice & Denis Conroy ?)
Mary Anne, June 1861 (Joseph Francis Flynn & Anne Dolan)

Peter Fitzmaurice & Anne Brehony
Thomas John, May 1856 (Patrick Judge & Debora Boland)
Patrick Michael, Sept. 1865 (civil record), Cherryfield

Note: mother's name was given as Mary in Patrick Michael's record.

Kate Fitzmaurice & Patrick Kedian
m. June 1856 (Thomas ? & ? Fitzmaurie), Annagh
Eleanor, June 1856 (Thomas Bride & J. Fitzmaurice) [date requires verification]

Sara (Sabina) Fitzmaurice & Patrick Frehilly
John, June 1856 (John Fitzmaurice & Catherine Fitzmaurice), Bekan

John Fitzmaurice & Peggy Waldron
David, Jan. 1857 (Michael Kyne & Bridget Nowlan), Bekan

Patrick Fitzmaurice & Ellen Dyer / Dwyer
m. Apr. 1857 (Thomas Fitzmaurice & Catherine Fitzmaurice), Bekan
James, Augt. 1860 (James Devine & Sarah Adams ?), Gorteenbeg
John, June 1864 (civil record)
Augustine, Augt. 1866 (Michael Higgins & Mary Greally)
Bridget, Oct. 1867 (civil record), Gorteen
Catherine, Nov. 1868 (Patrick Fitzmaurice & Anne Lyons)
Martin, Oct. 1870 (civil record)
Austin, Augt. 1876 (civil record)
Mary Ellen, Feb. 1881 (civil record)
Honor, March 1883 (civil record), Lisbaun
Anne, July 1888 (civil record; Ellen Dwyer of Gorteen present), Brackloon

Note: Patrick was the son of Martin Fitzmaurice of Derrynacong. He was the brother of John (married to Mary Greally) & Michael (married to Anne Lyons).

Eleanor Fitzmaurice & James Byrne
Dominick, Augt 1857 (Patrick Byrne & Sara Fitzmaurice), Bekan

Honor Fitzmaurice & John Cunnane
m. Nov. 1857 (James Fitzmaurice & Mary McHugh), Bekan
Michael, Feb. 1860 (James Fitzmaurice & Catherine Haddican)
Patrick, Nov. 1861 (Michael Cunnane & Maria Grogan)
John, Apr. 1863 (James Fitzmaurice & Bridget Fitzmaurice)

Note: the mother's name was given as Mary in Michael's record.

Michael Fitzmaurice & Catherine Dever [name requires verification]
Bridget Ellen, Feb. 1858 (Patrick Judge & Mary Lyons), Bekan

Michael Fitzmaurice & Honoria Dyer
m. Feb. 1858 (Timothy Fitzmaurice & Honor Hunt), Bekan
Mary, May 1860 (Timothy Fitzmaurice & Margaret Fitzmaurice)
Child, 1862 (Patrick Nowlan & Anne Flatley) [record requires verification]
Elizabeth, Apr. 1864 (Peter Fitzmaurice & Sabina Fitzmaurice), Forthill
Cecilia, Apr. 1864 twin (Mark Dyer & Honora Hunt)
Michael, May 1866 (Patrick Dyer & Bridget Fitzmaurice)
Timothy, Dec. 1868 (civil record)
Honoria, Apr. 1870 (Patrick Fitzmaurice & ??)
Catherine, Oct. 1874 (civil record)
Mark, March 1877 (civil record; Peter Fitzmaurice present)
Timothy, May 1880 (civil record; Eliza Fitzmaurice present)

Sara (Sabina) Fitzmaurice & Peter Waldron
Mary, Feb. 1859 (John Flatley & Bridget Fitzmaurice), Bekan
John, May 1861 (Thomas Waldron & Catherine Fitzmaurice)
Bridget, Oct. 1862 (Michael Waldron & Margaret Ruane)
Margaret, July 1864 (Philip Darcy & Bridget Darcy), Knockaunacat, Bekan
John, July 1867 (Timothy Flynn & Eleanor Fitzmaurice)

Thomas Fitzmaurice & Catherine McHale
m. March 1859 (Patrick Fitzmaurice & Margaret Dorey), Annagh [requires verification]
Mary, March 1861 (William Fitzmaurice), Leo
David, Dec. 1865 (civil record)
Thomas, Dec. 1867 (civil record)
Patrick, May 1870 (civil record)
Anne, Oct. 1872 (John Carney & Bridget Carney)
John, Feb. 1875 (Edward Murry & Deborah ?)
Kate, July 1877 (civil record)
Michael, Sept. 1878 (John Grogan & Elizabeth Grogan)
William, Sept. 1881 (civil record)
James Austin, Augt. 1884 (civil record; Patrick Fitzmaurice of Leo present)
Peter, Nov. 1886 (civil record; John Fitzmaurice of Leo present)

Catherine Fitzmaurice & Michael Morris
m. Apr. 1859 (John Sloyan & Mary Fitzmaurice), Bekan

Catherine Fitzmaurice & John ?
m. Apr. 1859 (Thomas Shaughnessy & Sarah Fitzmaurice), Annagh

Timothy Fitzmaurice & Catherine Fitzmaurice
Honoria, Nov. 1859 (Michael Fitzmaurice & Ellen Fitzmaurice)
Ellen, Jan. 1862 (John Fitzmaurice & Mary Fitzmaurice)
Catherine, Sept. 1864 (civil record), Forthill
Mary, Sept. 1866 (James Fitzmaurice & Ellen Fitzmaurice)
John Joseph, Jan. 1869 (John Fitzmaurice & Honoria Flatley)
Patrick, Sept. 1871 (civil record)
Timothy, Jan. 1874 (civil record)

Luke Fitzmaurice & Elizabeth Morley [name requires verification]
Honor ? 1859 (John Fitzmaurice & Mary Grogan), Annagh [date requires verification]

Kate Fitzmaurice & Anthony Morley
m. Jan. 1860 (E. Murray & ? Waldron), Annagh

Patrick Fitzmaurice & Bridget Kyne /Coyne
m. Apr. 1860 (? & ? Henecan), Annagh (record requires verification]
Mary, Feb. 1861 (James Carroll & Ellen Burke)
Thomas, Dec. 1862 (Ellen Fitzmaurice)
Michael, Sept. 1865 (John Kyne & Mary Kyne; Ellen Diskin present), Laughil
Catherine, Feb. 1867 (Michael Flynn & Mary Hunt; Catherine Murphy present)
Bridget, Jan. 1869 (Michael Lyons & Mary Discon)
Ellen, Oct. 1871 (James Kilraine & Mary Discon; Catherine Murphy present)
Sarah, Oct. 1873 (Thomas Winston & Bridget Fitzmaurice; Mary Fitzmaurice present)

Honora Fitzmaurice & Michael ?
Honny? (Henry?), 1860 (Martin McGuire & Mary ?), Annagh [requires verification]

John Fitzmaurice & Catherine Duffy
m. Jan. 1861 (no witnesses listed), Bekan
Bridget, Augt. 1862 (? Bailey & Bridget Duffy), Clydagh
Martin, Sept. 1865 (civil record)
Thomas, Dec. 1867 (civil record)
John, Nov. 1868 (Michael Duffy & Mary Fitzmaurice)
Michael, Oct. 1874 (civil record)
Augustine, July 1877 (civil record; Bridget Fitzmaurice present)

John Fitzmaurice & Anne Fitzmaurice
Bridget, Jan. 1861 (William Fitzmaurice & M. Hardicane ?), Bekan

Catherine Fitzmaurice & Patrick McDonnell
m. Feb. 1861 (Austin Grogan & Sarah Fitzmaurice), Bekan

Patrick Fitzmaurice & Bridget Vizar [name requires verification]
m. Apr. 1861 (John Henecan & Kate Henecan ?), Annagh

Patrick Fitzmaurice & ? Fitzmaurice
Elizabeth, July 1861 (so sponsors listed), Annagh

Mary Fitzmaurice & John Kyne
m. July 1861 (no witnesses listed), Anngh [record needs to be verified]

Patrick Fitzmaurice & Julia Flatley [name requires verification]
Bridget, Nov. 1861 (Martin Flatley & Bridget Flatley), Bekan

Patrick Fitzmaurice & ??
Peter, June 1862 (Thomas Fitzmaurice & Bridget Fitzmaurice), Bekan

Peter Fitzmaurice & Sara Waldron
Bridget, Oct. 1862 (Michael Waldron & Margaret Ruane), Bekan

Mary Fitzmaurice & Thomas Hunt
m. Feb. 1863 (John Hunt & Mary Flatley) [date requires verification]
William, Nov. 1864 (Patrick Fitzmaurice & Margaret Fitzmaurice), Brackloon
Thomas, Augt. 1867 (Thomas Waldron & Catherine Fitzmaurice), Lisbaun

Mary Fitzmaurice & James Glynn
m. June 1863 (James ? & Catherine Folliard), Tonregee

Sarah Fitzmaurice & Thomas Waldron
m. July 1863 (Martin Kelly & Bridget Grogan), Bekan
Honoria, Jan. 1866 (Patrick Waldron & Bridget Waldron), Ballyhaunis
John, July 1867 (Timothy Fitzmaurice & Ellen Fitzmaurice)
Catherine, Jan. 1870 (? Fitzmaurice & Mary H-)

Note: Sarah was the daughter of Martin Fitzmaurice & Honoria Fitzmaurice. Thomas was the son of Myles Waldron & Mary Fitzmaurice. Sarah's brother married Mary Hannon.

Patrick Fitzmaurice & Bridget Caulfield
Mary, Jan. 1864 (civil record), Barheen
Bridget, Oct. 1866 (civil record)
Elizabeth, Sept. 1868 (civil record)
Patrick, Feb. 1870 (civil record)
Walter, Jan. 1871 (John Duffy & Mary Bride)
Thomas, Dec. 1874 (John Fitzmaurice & Bridget Fitzmaurice)

Michael Fitzmaurice & Ann Lyons
Michael, Sept. 1864 (civil record), Spaddagh
Patrick, Feb. 1866 (civil record)
Mary, Oct. 1867 (civil record)
Timothy, Dec. 1868 (Patrick Fitzmaurice & Mary Han-)
Catherine, June 1869 (? Fitzmaurice & Bridget Waldron)
Margaret, July 1870 (civil record)
John, Oct. 1871 (John Tarpey & Mary ?)
Honora, Nov. 1872 (Patrick Fitzmaurice & Eleanor Dyer)
Bridget, Apr. 1874 (Michael Fitzmaurice & Mary Lydon)
Anne, Sept. 1875 (? & Mary Waldron) [record requires verification]
Ellen, June 1877 (Patrick Fitzmaurice & Mary Fitzmaurice)
Sarah, Apr. 1879 (civil record)
Elizabeth, Oct. 1880 (civil record)
James, Apr. 1882 (civil record; Margaret Lyons of Forthill present)
Martin, Sept. 1883 (civil record)
Thomas, Apr. 1887 (civil record)

Sarah Fitzmaurice & Patrick Kelly
m. Jan. 1865 (Patrick Kelly & Sally Fitzmaurice), Bekan

Note: Sarah, age 18, was the daughter of John Fitzmaurice of Lisbaun.
Patrick, age 38, was the son of John Kelly of Derrynacong.

Bridget Fitzmaurice & Patrick Kelly
m. Jan. 1865 (Thomas Flatley & Bridget Flatley), Bekan

Note: Bridget, age 23, was the daughter of John Fitzmaurice of Lisbaun.
Patrick, age 42, was the son of John Kelly of Killunaugher.

Bridget Fitzmaurice & Thomas McHugh
m. Feb. 1865 (Timothy Mullowney & Mary Fitzmaurice)

Note: Bridget, age 20, was the daughter of James Fitzmaurice of
Treanrevagh. Thomas was the son of John McHugh of (illegible).

John Fitzmaurice & Mary Jordan
m. Feb. 1865 (John Sloyan & Nancy Jordan), Aghamore
Anne, Oct. 1866 (civil record), Lisbaun
Thomas, Augt. 1868 (John Sloyan & Mary Fitzmaurice)

Note: John was the son of Thomas Fitzmaurice of Cloongawnagh. Mary was the daughter of Thomas Jordan of Annagh.

Catherine Fitzmaurice & John Green
m. Feb. 1865 (John Green & Mary Green), Kiltullagh
Michael, July 1870 (Michael Stretch & Mary Hussey), Pollanalty
Patrick, Feb. 1872 (Thomas Green & Bridget Hussey)

Note: Catherine was the daughter of Patrick Fitzmaurice of Pollanalty. John was the son of Michael Green of Pollanalty.

Mary Fitzmaurice & Patrick Murray / Murry
m. May 1865 (Francis Murray & Mary Frehily), Bekan
Mary, Apr. 1869 (James Ruane & Mary Ruane), Derrintogher
Thomas, Augt. 1873 (Thomas Ruane & Bridget Connolly)
Michael, Oct. 1875 (Michael Fitzmaurice & Celia Flatley), Bargarriff
Bridget, July 1877 (William ? & Mary ?), Derrintogher
James, July 1879 (James Mannion & Mary Ruane)

Note: Mary was the daughter of Peter Fitzmaurice of Forthill. Patrick, age 23, was the son of John Murray of Derrintogher.

Martin Fitzmaurice & Ellen Larkin
m. May 1865 (David Fitzmaurice & Ann Grealy), Kiltullagh
Patrick, March 1866 (Patrick Larkin & Mary Larkin), Coolatinny
Thomas, Dec. 1867 (civil record; Margaret Larkin present)
John, May 1869 (Michael Caulfield & Mary Larkin; Bridget Larkin of Commons present)

Note: Martin was the son of Thomas Fitzmaurice, dec'd., of Coolatinny. Ellen was the daughter of Patrick Larkin of Corlegan ?

Catherine Fitzmaurice & Denis Sloyan
Catherine, Augt. 1865 (David Fitzmaurice & Mary Fitzmaurice)

Michael Fitzmaurice & Mary Flatley
Michael, Nov. 1865 (David Flatley & Bridget Fitzmaurice), Bekan

Sara (Sally) Fitzmaurice & James Neary / Nary
m. Jan. 1866 (Timothy Cassidy & Ellen Moran), Bekan
Thomas, Nov. 1866 (David Fitzmaurice & Catherine Nary)
Mary, Nov. 1868 (Thomas Neary & Catherine Nary), Forthill

Note: Sara was the daughter of David Fitzmaurice of Mountain. James was
the son of Bernard Neary of Crossard, Aghamore.

John Fitzmaurice & Mary Grealy
Patrick, Feb. 1866 (Patrick Grealy & Honoria Grealy), Derrynacong
John, Sept. 1867 (civil record; Honoria Waldron of Derrynacong present)
Ellen, May 1869 (Thomas Ryan ? & Winifred Waldron)
Martin, June, 1871 (Michael Fitzmaurice & Mary Fitzmaurice)
Mary, Augt. 1873 (Patrick Fitzmaurice & Mary Fitzmaurice)
Honoria, March 1876 (Patrick Fitzmaurice & Mary Fitzmaurice)

Note: John Fitzmaurice was the son of Martin Fitzmaurice of Derrynacong.
His brothers were Patrick (married to Ellen Dwyer) & Michael (married to
Anne Lyons). John & Mary's civil marriage has not been located.

Catherine Fitzmaurice & Austin Caulfield
m. July 1866 (Thomas Caulfield & Catherine Fitzmaurice), Lugboy,
Ballindine
Kate, Apr. 1871 (Michael Fitzmaurice & Mary Fitzmaurice), Ballyhaunis
Bridget, June 1872 (Thomas Fitzmaurice & Mary Murphy)
Michael, May 1873 (William Meath & Kate Caulfield)
Ellen, May 1876 (Patrick McDonnell & Mary McDonnell)

Note: Catherine, age 22, was the daughter of John Fitzmaurice of Gorteen.
Austin, age 22, an egg buyer and shopkeeper, was the son of Patrick
Caulfield of Carrowkeel.

Patrick Fitzmaurice & Ellen Devine
Austin, Augt. 1866 (civil record), Gorteenbeg
Catherine, Oct. 1868 (civil record), Forthill
Patrick, July 1872 (civil record), Gorteenbeg
Michael, Oct. 1874 (civil record)

Bridget Fitzmaurice & Edmund Beasty
m. Feb. 1867 (Thomas Beasty & Mary Murphy), Annagh
Mary, March 1869 (Michael Fitzmaurice & Bridget C-), Pattenspark
James, Apr. 1872 (Patrick Beasty & Mary McDonnell)
Patrick, Augt. 1874 (Michael Fitzmaurice & Margaret Caulfield)
Bridget, March 1878 (Thomas Caulfield & Kate Fitzmaurice)
Edward, Apr. 1879 (James McDonnell & ? Caulfield)

Note: Bridget was the daughter of John Fitzmaurice of Gorteen. Edmund
was the son of John Beasty of Woodpark.

John Fitzmaurice & Mary Beasty
m. March 1867 (John Fitzmaurice & Maria Flaherty), Bekan

Note: John was the son of Thomas Fitzmaurice of Pattenspark. Mary was
the daughter of Patrick Beasty of Pattenspark.

Ellen Fitzmaurice & Martin Morley
m. Dec. 1867 (Patrick Fitzmaurice & Bridget Sloyan), Annagh
Kate, March 1871 (sponsors illegible), Barheen
John, June 1877 (John Morley & Kate Morley)

Note: Ellen was the daughter of John Fitzmaurice of Barheen. Martin was
the son of Anthony Morley of Barheen.

Michael Fitzmaurice & Mary Hussey
m. Feb. 1868 (John McQ- & Ellen Hussey), Kiltullagh

Note: Michael was the son of Patrick Fitzmaurice of Tonregee. Mary, a
widow, was the daughter of Thomas Hussey of Pollanalty.

David Fitzmaurice & Bridget Fitzmaurice
m. March 1868 (witnesses illegible)

Note: David was from Mountain. His father, name illegible, was decreased. Bridget, a widow, was the daughter of Thomas Kelly, dec'd., of Ballyhaunis.

Peter Fitzmaurice & Bridget Morley
m. Nov. 1868 (Patrick Naughton & Honor Morley), Bekan
Peter, Oct. 1869 (civil record; Patrick Judge of Cherryfield present), Cherryfield
Honoria, June 1871 (civil record; Bridget Morley of Bekan present)
Bridget, Feb. 1873 (civil record; Thomas Fitzmaurice of Cherryfield present)

Note: Peter, age 30, was the son of Patrick Fitzmaurice of Churchfield. Bridget, age 24, was the daughter of Edmund Morley of Cloonbulban.

Margaret Fitzmaurice & Thomas Healy
m. Feb. 1869 (Martin Healy & Catherine Fitzmaurice), Bekan
Thomas, Dec. 1870 (William ? & ? Fitzmaurice)

Note: Margaret was the daughter of William Fitzmaurice of Lisbaun. Thomas was the son of James Healy of Aghamore.

Margaret Fitzmaurice & Martin Hanon
m. Feb. 1869 (Peter Fitzmaurice & Mary Hanon)
Thomas, March 1870 (David Fitzmaurice & ? Flatley), Bekan

Note: Margaret was the daughter of Peter Fitzmaurice of Forthill. Martin was the son of Thomas Hanon, dec'd., of Togher.

Margaret Fitzmaurice & John Wynne
Thomas, Jan. 1870 (civil record), Abbeyquarter
Catherine, Nov. 1872 (Patrick ? & Bridget Concannon ?), Ballyhaunis
Edward, March 1877 (John Wynne & Kate Bligh)

Cecilia Fitzmaurice & Patrick Vasey [name requires verification]
James, Jan. 1870 (James ? & Ellen Fitzmaurice), Bekan

Peter Fitzmaurice & Margaret McGarry
m. Jan. 1870 (Timothy Fitzmaurice & Bridget Lyons), Bekan
Peter, Jan. 1871 (Timothy Fitzmaurice & Mary McGarry), Forthill
James, Apr. 1872 (civil record)
Mary, June 1874 (civil record), Clagnagh
Ellen, Dec. 1876 (civil record)
Andrew, Nov. 1878 (civil record)
Cecilia, Jan. 1881 (civil record), Ballyhaunis
Michael, Sept. 1882 (civil record)
Catherine, May 1884 (civil record)
John, Sept. 1886 (civil record)
Honoria, March 1889 (civil record)
Bridget, Jan. 1891 (civil record)
Margaret, July 1893 (civil record)
Anne, Nov. 1896 (civil record)

Note: Peter, a shopkeeper, was the son of Peter Fitzmaurice, dec'd., of Forthill. Margaret was the daughter of James McGarry of Clagnagh.

Sarah Fitzmaurice & James Waldron
Catherine, Jan. 1870 (Timothy Fitzmaurice & ?), Ballyhaunis

Mary Fitzmaurice & Thomas Finnegan
m. Jan. 1870 (Thomas Finnegan & Catherine Fitzmaurice), Bekan
James, June 1870 (Michael Conway & Mary Jordan), Knockbrack
Patrick, Oct. 1875 (Patrick Gordon & Anne Fitzgerald)

Note: Mary was the daughter of William Fitzmaurice of Lisbaun. Thomas was the son of John Finnegan, dec'd., of Corrasluastia.

Bridget Fitzmaurice & John Burke
m. Feb. 1870 (Patrick McLoughlin & Margaret Byrne), Bekan

Note: Bridget was the daughter of James Fitzmaurice, dec'd, of Reask. John was the son of William Burke, dec'd., of Lakehill ?

John Fitzmaurice & Catherine Greally
m. Feb. 1870 (Michael Fitzmaurice & Bridget Greally), Bekan
Sarah, Dec. 1871 (civil record), Lisbaun
Child, Feb. 1876 (civil record)

Note: John was the son of John Fitzmaurice, dec'd., of Lisbaun. Catherine was the daughter of Thomas Greally of Forthill.

David Fitzmaurice & Mary Hannon
m. Feb. 1870 (Timothy Fitzmaurice & Sara Anne Cullen), Bekan
Catherine, Dec. 1870 (Martin Hannon & Margaret Hannon) Togher
Mary Ellen, Apr. 1872 (civil record)
Honoria, Sept. 1873 (civil record; Catherine Hannon present)
Michael Austin, Sept. 1875 (civil record)
Thomas, Sept. 1877 (civil record)
David, Augt. 1879 (civil record)
Martin, Oct. 1881 (civil record; Martin Hannon of Togher present)
Timothy, Jan. 1883 (civil record)
Sara, Augt. 1887 (civil record; Kate Fitzmaurice present)

Note: David was the son of Martin Fitzmaurice, dec'd., of Togher. Mary was the daughter of Thomas Hannon, dec'd., of Togher.

Cecilia Fitzmaurice & Henry Mannion
m. March 1870 (Michael Grogan & Margaret Kelly), Annagh
John, Jan. 1871 (John Mannion & Michael ? Fitzmaurice), Lisduff
Thomas, Nov, 1873 (Luke Mannion & Anne Godfrey)
Mary, Feb. 1875 (civil record), Lisduff

Note: Cecilia was the daughter of Thomas Fitzmaurice of Lisduff. Henry was the son of John Mannion of Drumbaun.

Patrick Fitzmaurice & Honor Fitzmaurice
m. Apr. 1870 (Martin Coyne & Ellen Fitzmaurice), Aghamore Parish

Mary, 1872 (civil record), Tonregee
Patrick, Jan. 1874 (civil record)
Thomas, Apr. 1876 (Michael Fitzmaurice & Mary Kirrane)
John, May 1880 (Thomas Kelly & Mary Fitzmaurice)
John, May 1889 (civil record)

Note: Patrick, age 30, was the son of John Fitzmaurice of Tonregee. Honor, age 22, was the daughter of Patrick Fitzmaurice of Culnacleha.

Patrick Fitzmaurice & ??
Peter, Nov. 1870 (Edward Morley & ??), Bekan

Bridget Fitzmaurice & David Flatley
m. Feb. 1871 (Patrick Flatley & Mary Flatley), Bekan
Mary Anne, Feb. 1881 (civil record), Forthill

Note: Bridget was the daughter of David Fitzmaurice of Brackloon. David was the son of William Flatley of Forthill.

Thomas Fitzmaurice & Bridget Hunt
m. March 1871 (Timothy Fitzmaurice & Bridget Hunt), Bekan

Note: Thomas was the son of Patrick Fitzmaurice, dec'd., of Culnacleha. Bridget was the daughter of James Hunt of Scregg.

David Fitzmaurice & Bridget Waldron
m. Apr. 1871 (Thomas Caulfield & Mary Feeny ?)
Mary, Apr. 1872 (civil record; Mary Fitzmaurice of Mountain present)
John, Apr. 1874 (civil record), Mountain

Note: David was the son of Thomas Fitzmaurice, dec'd., of Mountain. Bridget was the daughter of Francis Waldron of Arderrig ?

Patrick Fitzmaurice & Margaret McNamara
m. Feb. 1872 (Patrick Fitzmaurice & Catherine Fitzmaurice), Bekan
Mary, Feb. 1873 (civil record; Margaret Healy of Lisbaun present), Brackloon

Patrick, Feb. 1875 (civil record), Lisbaun
Child, Dec. 1876 (civil record)

Note: Patrick was the son of William Fitzmaurice of Lisbaun. Margaret was the daughter of Patrick McNamara of Brackloon.

Catherine Fitzmaurice & Michael Leonard
John, May 1872 (Patrick Flatley & Ellen Fitzmaurice)
Hubert, Augt. 1873 (James Leonard & Bridget Connell), Redhill
Thomas, Augt. 1876 (Thomas Fitzmaurice & Catherine Fitzmaurice), Carrickacat

David Fitzmaurice & Kate Feeny
Ellen, June 1872 (no sponsors listed), Annagh [record requires verification]

Patrick Fitzmaurice & Mary Carney
m. Jan. 1873 (Martin Fitzmaurice & Ellen Currane), Bekan
James, Dec. 1873 (civil record), Reask
Bridget, Sept. 1875 (civil record)
Martin, Feb. 1877 (civil record)
Mary, Apr. 1879 (civil record)
Catherine, Jan. 1881 (civil record)
Anne, Sept. 1882 (civil record; Honoria Forde of Reask present)
Ellen, Nov. 1884 (civil record)
Margaret, Augt. 1886 (civil record)
Patrick, Feb. 1889 (civil record)
John, Dec.1893 (civil record)

Note: Patrick was the son of James Fitzmaurice, dec'd., of Reask. Mary was the daughter of Anthony Carney of Ballindrehid.

Mary Fitzmaurice & Patrick Hart
m. Feb. 1873 (James Waldron & Anne Hunt), Bekan

Note: Mary was the daughter of Mark Fitzmaurice of Forthill. Patrick was the son of Peter Hart of Brackloon.

Mary Fitzmaurice & Patrick Boyle
m. Feb. 1873 (Patrick ? & Bridget Fitzmaurice), Bekan

Note: Mary was the daughter of Peter Fitzmaurice of Larganboy. Patrick was the son of Michael Boyle, dec'd., of Kilgarriff, Aghamore.

John Fitzmaurice & Bridget Fitzmaurice
m. March 1873 (John Burke & Ellen Fitzmaurice), Bekan

Note: John was the son of Patrick Fitzmaurice, dec'd., of Culnacleha. Bridget was the daughter of John Fitzmaurice, dec'd., of Gorteen More.

Ellen Fitzmaurice & Denis Forde
m. March 1873 (Thomas Rattigan & Bridget Kenny), Annagh
Charles Patrick, Feb. 1874 (James O'Malley & Mary Fitzmaurice), Ballyhaunis
Denis Austin, Augt. 1875 (Michael Mulkinney ? & Honor Fitzmaurice)
Elizabeth, March 1877 (Patrick Freely & Honora Fitzmaurice)
Denis, March 1879 (Thomas Lyons & Cecilia Lyons)
Patrick, March 1881 (John Fitzmaurice & Anne O'Malley)
Mary, March 1883 (Patrick Forde & Honora Forde)
Denis, Jan. 1886 (? Golden & M. Godfrey)

Note: Ellen, age 17, was the daughter of Patrick Fitzmaurice, dec'd., of Ballyhaunis. Denis, a publican, was the son of Charles Forde of Ballyhaunis.

Martin Fitzmaurice & Catherine McHugh
m. June 1873 (Patrick Lyons & Bridget Concannon), Bekan
John, Apr. 1874 (civil record), Bekan
Bridget, Jan. 1876 (civil record), Treanrevagh
Patrick, March 1880 (civil record Thomas McHugh present)
Margaret, May 1883 (civil record)
Celia, Augt. 1887 (civil record)
Anne, July 1889 (civil record; Bridget Higgins present)

Note: Martin was the son of James Fitzmaurice of Treanrevagh. Catherine was the daughter of John McHugh of Ballygatha ?

Mary Anne Fitzmaurice & Patrick Maughan
m. Oct. 1873 (John Waldron & Catherine McDonnell), Bekan

Note: Mary Anne was the daughter of John Fitzmaurice of Lisbaun. Patrick was the son of John Maughan of Lisbaun.

Thomas Fitzmaurice & Honor Kneafsy
m. Feb. 1874 (Patrick Fitzmaurice & Mary Lyons), Bekan
Bridget, Dec. 1874 (civil record), Forthill
Mark, March 1876 (civil record)
Patrick, Augt. 1882 (civil record)
Thomas, Feb. 1886 (civil record)

Note: Thomas was the son of Mark Fitzmaurice & Bridget Hunt of Forthill. Honor was the daughter of Patrick Kneafsy of Erriff.

Mary Fitzmaurice & John Henry
m. Sept. 1874 (Thomas Cassidy & Margaret Doyle), Annagh

Note: Mary, a dressmaker, was the daughter of Myles Fitzmaurice of Ballyhaunis. John was the son of Thomas Henry of Gorteen, "late of Church St., Bolton."

Michael Fitzmaurice & Bridget Raftery
m. Feb. 1875 (Michael Ryan & Catherine Raftery) Kiltullagh
Mary, Feb. 1876 (Thomas Raftery & Bridget Raftery), Gorteen
Catherine, Oct. 1877 (James Mulquin & Mary Raftery)
Bridget, Sept. 1879 (John Fitzmaurice & Bridget Fitzmaurice)
John, Oct. 1881 (civil record)
Thomas, Apr. 1884 (civil record)
Patrick, July 1886 (civil record)
Michael, Jan. 1889 (civil record,
Bridget, Apr. 1891 (civil record)
James, June, 1893 (civil record)
Martin, June 1895 (civil record)

Genealogical Troves ~ Volume Three

Note: Michael, age 25, was the son of John Fitzmaurice of Gorteen. Bridget, age 20, was the daughter of James Raftery of Tonregee.

Michael Fitzmaurice & Mary Fitzmaurice
m. March 1875 (Michael Waldron & Anne Hussey), Kiltullagh

Note: Michael was the son of John Fitzmaurice of Tonregee. Mary, a widow, was the daughter of Thomas Hussey of Pollanarroo, Kiltullagh.

Thomas Fitzmaurice & Bridget Gordon
m. Dec. 1875 (James Fitzmaurice & Bridget Halligan), Knock

Note: Thomas, age 26, was the son of James Fitzmaurice of Woods ? Bridget, age 21, was the daughter of James Gordon of Bohauns.

John Fitzmaurice & Bridget Waldron
m. Jan. 1876 (Timothy Fitzmaurice & Mary Waldron), Bekan
Michael, Dec. 1876 (civil record), Mountain
Timothy, Augt. 1879 (civil record)
Timothy Martin, Nov. 1881 (civil record)

Note: John was the son of John Fitzmaurice of Forthill. Bridget was the daughter of Francis Waldron of Mountain.

Mary Fitzmaurice & Michael Loftus
m. Feb. 1876 (John Loftus & Celia Fitzmaurice), Annagh

Note: Mary was the daughter of Patrick Fitzmaurice of Woodpark. Michael was the son of Michael Loftus, dec'd., of Johnstown.

Catherine Fitzmaurice & James Waldron
m. Feb. 1876 (Patrick Tully & Catherine Lyons), Annagh
Bridget, Apr. 1877 (Thomas Connell & Catherine Tully), Derrynacong
Mary, Augt. 1878 (Patrick Dyer & Catherine Tully)
John, Feb. 1880 (Michael Kedian & Honora Waldron)
James, Sept. 1882 (Patrick Fitzmaurice & Kate Bones)
Catherine, Oct. 1884 (Patrick Fitzmaurice & Mary Kelly)

101

Honoria, Oct. 1886 (John Fitzmaurice & Mary Hunt)
Patrick, June 1889 (Patrick Fitzmaurice & Kate Lynskey)

Note: Catherine was the daughter of Patrick Fitzmaurice & Mary Waldron of Derrynacong. James was the son of James Waldron & Catherine Dyer of Brackloon.

Timothy Fitzmaurice & Mary Lyons
m. Nov. 1876 (John Fitzmaurice & Maggie Lyons), Bekan
Mary Ellen, Oct. 1877 (civil record; Margaret Hannon present), Ballyhaunis
Margaret, Apr. 1879 (civil record; Sara McHugh present)
Delia Kate, July 1883 (civil record; Bridget Walsh present)
Maggie Jane, Augt. 1884 (civil record; Maggie Walsh of Claremorris present)

Timothy, a "dealer" and publican, was the son of Peter Fitzmaurice, dec'd., of Ballyhaunis. Mary was the daughter of Bernard Lyons, dec'd., of Cloonacurry.

Mary Fitzmaurice & John Fahey
m. Dec. 1876 (Michael Higgins & Mary Higgins), Bekan

Note: Mary was the daughter of Michael Fitzmaurice of Brackloon. John was the son of John Fahey of Tulrohaun, Annagh.

John Fitzmaurice & Mary Culliney
m. Dec. 1876 (John Grealy & Margaret Culliney), Bekan
John, March 1881 (civil record), Lisbaun
Mary, Dec. 1883 (civil record)
Mary, Feb. 1886 (civil record)
James, March 1888 (civil record)
Kate, Jan. 1890 (civil record)
Maggie Jane, Apr. 1892 (civil record)
Michael, July 1894 (civil record)
Sara, Feb. 1897 (civil record)

Note: John was the son of John Fitzmaurice of Lisbaun. Mary was the daughter of James Culliney of Lassanny.

Patrick Fitzmaurice & Mary Fitzmaurice
m. Feb. 1877 (Patrick Fitzmaurice & Margaret Fitzmaurice), Bekan
John Thomas, July 1881 (civil record), Ballyhaunis
Patrick, Sept. 1884 (civil record; Catherine Fitzmaurice of Kilmannin present)
Child, Feb. 1889 (civil record)
Margaret, Feb. 1891 (civil record), Hazelhill
Michael, July 1892 (civil record), Ballyhaunis

Note: Patrick, a shoemaker, was the son of Patrick Fitzmaurice of Barheen. Mary was the daughter of John Fitzmaurice of Kilmannin.

John Charles Fitzmaurice & Elizabeth Forde
m. Feb. 1877 (Dominick Andrew Cullen & Mary Fitzmaurice)

Note: John Charles, a carpenter, was the son of Patrick Fitzmaurice of Ballyhaunis. Elizabeth was the daughter of Charles Forde of Ballyhaunis.

Catherine Fitzmaurice & John Higgins
Michael, July 1877 (James Neenan & Mary Fitzmaurice), Corrasluastia

Mary Fitzmaurice & Patrick Moore
Mary Ellen, Augt. 1877 (Michael Connell & Ellen Kelly), Derrynacong
Honora, Augt. 1877 twin (Thomas Waldron & Anne Moore)
Patrick, Augt. 1877 twin (civil record, Catherine Wadron informant)

Note: Patrick Moore died Jan. 1877, age given as 29 (Garraun, Catherine Waldron of Derrynacong, informant). Patrick Jr. died, one day of age, in August. Mary Ellen & Honoria died, one month of age, in October. No marriage record has been located.

Thomas Fitzmaurice & Mary Kyne / Coyne
m. Sept. 1877 (Bridget Judge & Michael Dwyer), Kiltullagh
Anne, Sept. 1878 (Bryan Kyne & Bridget Kyne)
Michael, July 1880 (civil record), Devlis
Patrick, Augt. 1882 (civil record)

Note: Thomas, age 21 and a railway officer, was the son of Peter Fitzmaurice of Cherryfield. Mary, age 21, was the daughter of Farrell Coyne of Clooncrim.

James Fitzmaurice & Catherine Feeny
m. Feb. 1878 (Michael Caulfield & Ellen Feeny), Annagh
Mary Ellen, Jan. 1879 (Thomas Feeny & Ellen Feeny), Derrylea
Margaret, July 1881 (civil record)
James, July 1888 (civil record)
Michael Martin, Dec. 1890 (civil record)
John, Apr. 1893 (civil record)
Kate, May 1896 (civil record)
Delia, Augt. 1898 (civil record; Patrick Fitzmaurice of Derrylea present)

Note: James was the son of James Fitzmaurice of Treanrevagh. Catherine was the daughter of Michael Feeny of Derrylea.

Honoria Fitzmaurice & Thomas Byrne
m. Feb. 1878 (Edmund Judge & Celia Fitzmaurice), Annagh
Cecilia, Jan. 1879 (Thomas Fitzmaurice & Sara Feely ?), Lisduff

Note: Honoria was the daughter of Thomas Fitzmaurice of Lisduff. Thomas, a cooper, was the son of Patrick Byrne of Lisduff.

Ellen Fitzmaurice & Patrick Waldron
m. Feb. 1879 (Peter Waldron & Mary Flatley), Bekan

Note: Ellen was the daughter of John Fitzmaurice of Forthill. Patrick was the son of Thomas Waldron of illegible, possibly Gortnageeragh, Annagh.

Bridget Fitzmaurice & Owen Lavin
m. Feb. 1879 (Michael Lee & Bridget Veasy), Bekan

Note: Bridget was the daughter of Peter Fitzmaurice of Larganboy. Owen was the son of Dominick Lavin of Kilgarriff, Aghamore.

Mary Fitzmaurice & James Connelly
m. March 1879 (Michael Morley & Mary Brennan), Bekan

Note: Mary was the daughter of Peter Fitzmaurice of Clagnagh. James was the son of David ? Connelly of Holywell.

Mary Fitzmaurice & Michael Nolan
m. Feb. 1880 (Patrick Waldron & Catherine Kedian), Bekan

Note: Mary was the daughter of David Fitzmaurice of Mountain. Michael was the son of Owen Nolan of Mountain.

Thomas Fitzmaurice & Sara Anne Grogan
m. March 1880 (James McTigue & ? Lyons), Annagh
Mary, Jan. 1881 (civil record), Classaghroe
James, June 1884 (civil record; Mary Finn of Ballyhaunis present)
Kate, June 1886 (civil record; Mary Finn of Tawnaghmore present)
David, June 1888 (civil record; Bridget Grealy of Ballyhaunis present), Ballyhaunis
Sara, Nov. 1892 (civil record)
Thomas, Nov 1892 twin (civil record)

Note: civil record of marriage not found. Thomas was described as a shopkeeper in Kate's record and as being in America in Mary's record.

Elizabeth Fitzmaurice & Thomas Boyle
m. Feb. 1881 (Patrick Conboy & Margaret Fitzmaurice), Bekan

Note: Elizabeth was the daughter of Mark Fitzmaurice of Forthill. Thomas, a widower, was the son of James Boyle of Killunaugher.

John Fitzmaurice & Catherine Lyons
m. March 1881 (Andrew Fitzmaurice & Bridget Lyons), Bekan
Bridget, Jan. 1883 (civil record), Brackloon
Margaret, Feb. 1887 (civil record)
Honny, Sept. 1892 (civil record)
Mary, Jan. 1896 (civil record)

Sara Teresa, Nov. 1898 (civil record)
Michael, March 1899 (civil record), Forthill
Patrick, Jan. 1900 (civil record; Mary Fitzmaurice of Brackloon present)
Catherine, Dec. 1900 (civil record)
Kate, Feb. 1901 (civil record; Bridget Fitzmaurice of Brackloon present)

Note: John was the son of David Fitzmaurice of Brackloon. Catherine was the daughter of John Lyons of Lurgan.

Celia Fitzmaurice & Patrick Eagney
m. June 1881 (Patrick Kenny & Mary Connolly), Annagh

Note: Celia was the daughter of Patrick Fitzmaurice of Woodpark. Patrick was the son of Patrick Eagney, dec'd., of Hollywell Lower.

Mark Fitzmaurice & Catherine Finn
Patrick, June 1881 (civil record), Barheen
Mary, Apr. 1883 (civil record; Mary Fitzmaurice, grandmother, present)

Margaret Fitzmaurice & Thomas Hunt
m. Feb. 1882 (John Hunt & Honora Fitzmaurice), Bekan

Note: Margaret was the daughter of Thomas Fitzmaurice of Brackloon. Thomas was the son of John Hunt of Cloonbook.

Mary Fitzmaurice & Patrick Byrne
m. March 1883 (John Byrne & Mary Veasy), Bekan
Ellen, Jan. 1889 (civil record), Reask

Note: Mary, age 30, was the daughter of Patrick Fitzmaurice of Reask. Patrick, age 32, was the son of Thomas Byrne of Balaroe ?

Thomas Fitzmaurice & Bridget Waldron
m. Apr. 1883 (Thomas Waldron & Mary Anne Waldron), Kiltullagh
Nannie, Nov. 1886 (civil record), Cloonfad
Luke, Apr. 1888 (civil record)
Thomas Alfred, May 1893 (civil record)

Sara Teresa, May 1895 (civil record)
John Joseph, Sept. 1896 (civil record)

Note: Thomas, a national school teacher, was the son of Michael Fitzmaurice of Forthill. Bridget, also a national school teacher, was the daughter of Luke Waldron of Cloonfad.

Patrick Fitzmaurice & Bridget Waldon
m. June 1883 (Austin Lyons & Hannah Hallon ?), Bekan

Note: Patrick, age 40 and a widower, was the son of Patrick Fitzmaurice, dec'd., of Barheen. Bridget, age 35, was the daughter of John Waldron of Derrymore.

Timothy Fitzmaurice & Honor Flatley
m. Feb. 1884 (James Regan & Bridget Walsh), Annagh

Note: Timothy was the son of Martin Fitzmaurice, dec'd., of Ballyhaunis. Honor was the daughter of Andrew Flatley, dec'd., of Barheen.

Mary Fitzmaurice & Patrick McDonagh
m. Apr. 1884 (Thomas Hoban & Bridget Waldron), Bekan
Anne, March 1900 (civil record), Grallagh Garden

Note: Mary, age 20, was the daughter of Patrick Fitzmaurice of Lisbaun. Patrick was the son of Patrick McDonagh, dec'd., of Lisbaun.

Bridget Fitzmaurice & Thomas Curley
John, July 1884 (John Fitzmaurice & Honora Fitzmaurice), Derrynacong

Mary Fitzmaurice & Matthew McGuire
m. Augt. 1884 (James McGuire & Kitty ? Fitzmaurice), Knock

Note: Mary was the daughter of Patrick Fitzmaurice, dec'd., of Culnacleha. Matthew was the son of Thomas McGuire, dec'd., of Brackloon.

Mary Fitzmaurice & John Greally
m. Sept. 1884 (Patrick Culliney & Elizabeth Fitzmaurice), Bekan
Mark, Sept. 1900 (civil record), Mountain

Note: Mary was the daughter of Michael Fitzmaurice of Forthill. John was the son of Thomas Greally of Mountain.

Andrew Fitzmaurice & Bridget Flatley
m. March 1885 (Thomas Hoban & Catherine Flatley), Bekan
Mary Ellen, Feb. 1886 (civil record; Honny Fitzmaurice present), Brackloon
Honny, Sept. 1887 (civil record)
Kate, Sept. 1888 (civil record)
Bridget, Nov. 1890 (civil record)
John Francis, May 1893 (civil record)
Michael, March 1895 (civil record)
Andrew, Jan. 1897 (civil record)
James, June 1898 (civil record; Mary Devany of Brackloon present)
William, Nov. 1900 (civil record; Mary Ellen Fitzmaurice of Brackloon present)

Note: Andrew was the son of Thomas Fitzmaurice of Brackloon North. Bridget was the daughter of Dominick Flatley of Gorteen More.

Ellen Fitzmaurice & Thomas Duffy
m. Jan. 1886 (Michael Duffy & Honny Fitzmaurice), Knock

Note: Ellen was the daughter of Timothy Fitzmaurice of Shanvaghera. Thomas was the son of Michael Duffy of Aghtaboy, Knock.

Patrick Fitzmaurice & Margaret Tuohey
m. Jan. 1888 (Thomas Coyne & Catherine Kenny), Aghamore

Note: Patrick was the son of Richard Fitzmaurice of Kilmovee. Margaret was the daughter of Patrick Tuohey of Falleighter.

Honoria Fitzmaurice & John W. Gilmore
m. Augt. 1888 (William Gilmore & Sarah English), Ballyhaunis

Note: Honoria, age 25, was the daughter of Patrick Fitzmaurice of Ballyhaunis. John, age 29, was the son of William Gilmore of Ballyhaunis.

Mark Fitzmaurice & Bridget Forkin
m. Jan. 1889 (Martin Devany & Mary Culling ?), Bekan
Catherine, Nov. 1889 (civil record, Mary Fitzmaurice present), Barheen
Child, Dec. 1891 (civil record)
Child, Apr. 1893 (civil record)
Child, Dec. 1894 (civil record)
Child, Sept. 1896 (civil record)
Bridget, June 1898 (civil record)

Note: Mark, a widower, was the son of Patrick Fitzmaurice, dec'd., of Barheen. Bridget was the daughter of Michael Forkin, dec'd., of Tawnaghmore.

Catherine Fitzmaurice & Thomas Murphy
m. March 1889 (John Murphy & Mary Fitzmaurice), Annagh

Note: Catherine was the daughter of Michael Fitzmaurice of Cloonascrat ? Thomas was the son of John Murphy, dec'd., of Killunaugher.

Honoria Fitzmaurice & Michael Coen
m. May 1890 (John Flatley & Kate Fitzmaurice), Knock

Note: Honoria was the daughter of Timothy Fitzmaurice of Shanvaghera. Michael was the son of Michael Coen of Erriff.

Mary Fitzmaurice & Michael Regan
m. Jan. 1891 (Francis Regan & Mary Fitzmaurice), Annagh
Patrick, July 1892 (Patrick Fitzmaurice & Mary Regan), Derrynacong
Mary, Oct. 1894 (civil record; Patrick Fitzmaurice, grandfather, present)
Michael, Sept. 1897 (Patrick Fitzmaurice & Mary Anne Finnegan)

Note: Mary was the daughter of Patrick Fitzmaurice of Derrynacong. Michael was the son of Patrick Regan of Killunaugher. Mary married Thomas Ganley in the United States.

John Charles Fitzmaurice & Margaret McDermott
m. April 1891 (John Gilmore & Bridget McDermott)
Francis Patrick, Sept. 1893 (civil record; Bridget McDermott present), Ballyhaunis
Mary, Jan. 1895 (civil record)
John Charles, May 1897 (civil record)

Note: John Charles, a widower and carpenter, was the son of Patrick Fitzmaurice of Ballyhaunis. Margaret was the daughter of Bernard McDermott of Ballyhaunis.

John Fitzmaurice & Margaret Tarpey
m. Sept. 1891 (Edward Beasty & Lizzie Tarpey), Bekan

Note: John, a widower, was the son of Thomas Fitzmaurice of Holywell. Margaret was the daughter of Edward Tarpey of Bekan.

Elizabeth Fitzmaurice & Francis Flanagan
m. June 1892 (Peter Flatley & Honoria Fitzmaurice), Bekan

Note: Elizabeth was the daughter of Michael Fitzmaurice of Forthill. Francis was the son of Michael Flanagan, dec'd., of Ballindrehid.

Patrick Fitzmaurice & Kate Greally
John Patrick, Dec. 1892 (civil record), Kilmannin
Delia, Oct. 1893 (civil record), Ballyhaunis
Thomas, Dec. 1894 (civil record), Kilmannin
Michael, Apr. 1897 (civil record)
Kate Anne, Nov. 1898 (civil record)
James Martin, Feb. 1900 (civil record)

Note: the record of the marriage has not been located.

Kate Fitzmaurice & Patrick Coen
m. March 1894 (Thomas Fitzmaurice & Maria Ganley), Knock

Note: Kate was the daughter of Timothy Fitzmaurice of Shanvaghera. Patrick was the son of Michael Coen of Bruff, Aghamore.

Thomas Fitzmaurice & Catherine Sweeney
m. Feb. 1895 (Thomas Mannion & Anne Sweeney), Aghamore
Bridget, Nov. 1895 (civil record; Ellen Sweeney present), Lisduff
Thomas, Dec. 1898 (civil record)

Note: Thomas, age 26, was the son of Thomas Fitzmaurice of Lisduff. Catherine, age 25, was the daughter of Michael Sweeney of Ballynacloy, Aghamore.

John Fitzmaurice & Catherine Lyons
m. March 1895 (Michael Fitzmaurice & Mary Anne Lowry), Bekan

Note: the record of the marriage has not been located.

Patrick Fitzmaurice & Mary Reilly
m. March 1896 (James Fitzmaurice & Bridget Ganley)
Mary Anne, July 1898 (civil record), Tawnaghmore
Maggie Ellen, Nov. 1899 (civil record)
Thomas, Dec. 1900 (civil record)

Note: Patrick was the son of Patrick Fitzmaurice of Tawnaghmore. Mary was the daughter of Thomas Reilly of Holywell.

Mary Fitzmaurice & John Lyons
m. Augt. 1897 (Austin Lyons & Bridget Lyons), Bekan
Patrick, March 1900 (civil record), Greenwood

Note: Mary, age 24, was the daughter of Michael Fitzmaurice of Forthill. John, age 35, was the son of Patrick Lyons of Greenwood.

Ellen Fitzmaurice & John Murphy
m. Feb. 1898 (Michael Connor & Kate Fitzmaurice), Annagh
Bridget Agnes, Jan. 1900 (civil record), Killunaugher
Mary, June 1901 (civil record)

Catherine, Augt. 1905 (civil record; Mary Fitzmaurice present), Derrynacong
Ellen, Nov. 1906 (Michael McDonagh & Maggie Ryan)
Nora, Feb. 1908 (Patrick McDonagh & Mary McDonagh)
Anne, Apr. 1912 (civil record)

Note: Ellen, age 28, was the daughter of John Fitzmaurice of Derrynacong.
John, age 27, was the son of James Murphy of Killunaugher.

James Fitzmaurice & Honoria Clarke
m. March 1899 (Andrew Fitzmaurice & Honoria Killeen), Aghamore
Peter, Dec. 1899 (civil record), Tawnaghmore
Kate, July 1901 (civil record)

Note: James, age 27, was the son of Peter Fitzmaurice, shopkeeper, of
Tawnaghmore. Honora, age 30, was the daughter of Patrick Clarke of
Crossard.

Peter Fitzmaurice & Ellen Murphy
m. Apr. 1899 (Martin Crinigan ? & Mary Morley), Bekan
Mary, March 1900 (civil record), Cherryfield
John Thomas, Apr. 1901 (civil record)

Note: Peter was the son of Peter Fitzmaurice of Cherryfield. Ellen was the
daughter of William Murphy of Lissaniska.

Mary Fitzmaurice & Patrick Tarpey
Honoria, Feb. 1900 (civil record), Ballyhaunis

Note: Patrick was described as a shopkeeper.

John Charles Fitzmaurice & Mary Waldron
m. July 1900 (Nicholas Crosbie, Monica Waldron, Martha Waldron)
Elizabeth, Oct. 1901 (civil record; Mary Killeen of Ballyhaunis present),
Bekan

Note: John Charles, a carpenter and widower, was the son of Patrick Fitzmaurice of Ballyhaunis. Mary was the daughter of John Waldron of Devlis.

Norah Fitzmaurice & Michael Flatley
m. May 1901 (Martin Caulfield & Kate Fitzmaurice), Bekan

Note: Norah was the daughter of Michael Fitzmaurice of Forthill. Michael was the son of Martin Flatley of Lisbaun.

Augustine Fitzmaurice & Margaret Winston
John Thomas, Augt. 1901 (civil record; Catherine Fitzmaurice present), Clydagh

John Fitzmaurice & Ellen Flatley
m. March 1902 (Martin Fitzmaurice & Catherine Walsh), Bekan
Mary Agnes, July 1903 (Thomas Flatley & ? Fitzmaurice)
John, July 1905 (John Murphy & Bridget Flatley)
Bridget, Sept. 1906 (Martin Fitzmaurice & Ellen Waldron)
Ellen, Nov. 1908 (Martin Grogan & Daniel F-)
Rose Anne, March 1910 (Patrick Regan & Mary Fitzmaurice)
Nora, Feb. 1912 (Thomas Ganley & ? Ganley)
Margaret, Sept. 1913 (James Paisley & Joseph Paisley)

Note: John was the son of John Fitzmaurice of Derrynacong. Ellen was the daughter of William Flatley of Lassanny.

Michael Fitzmaurice & Sarah Boyle
m. March 1902 (John Fitzmaurice & Anne Murphy), Annagh

Note: Michael was the son of Patrick Fitzmaurice of Togher. Sarah was the daughter of Michael Boyle of Carrowneden.

Peter Fitzmaurice & Nora Hunt
m. May 1902 (Michael Fitzmaurice & Lizzie Hunt), Annagh

Note: Peter was the son of Michael Fitzmaurice of Forthill. Nora was the daughter of James Hunt of Scregg.

Nora Fitzmaurice & Thomas Flatley
m. June 1903 (Willie Flatley & Ellen Ryan), Bekan

Note: Nora was the daughter of John Fitzmaurice of Derrylahan. Thomas was the son of William Flatley of Lassanny.

David Fitzmaurice & Bridget Rogers
m. Augt. 1903 (Wm. Fitzmaurice & B. Henaghan), Annagh

Note: David was the son of John Fitzmaurice of Leo. Bridget was the daughter of Patrick Rogers of Tullaghaun.

Michael Fitzmaurice & Kate Freeley
m. May 1904 (Thomas Healey & Ellen Freeley), Bekan

Note: Michael was the son of Michael Fitzmaurice of Forthill. Kate was the daughter of John Freeley of Brackloon.

Kate Fitzmaurice & Andrew Flatley
m. July 1904 (Bernard Neary ? & Maggie J. Fitzmaurice), Annagh

Note: Kate was the daughter of Michael Fitzmaurice of Ballyhaunis. Andrew was the son of Peter Flatley of Forthill.

Norah Fitzmaurice & James Culliney
m. Feb. 1906 (James Fitzmaurice & Ellen Fitzmaurice), Annagh

Note: Norah was the daughter of Michael Fitzmaurice of Spaddagh. James was the son of James Culliney, dec'd., of Lassanny.

Patrick Fitzmaurice & Elizabeth Dyer
m. March 1906 (Michael Flanagan & Delia Dyer), Bekan

Note: Patrick was the son of Patrick Fitzmaurice of Lisbaun. Elizabeth was the daughter of Mark Dyer of Brackloon.

Martin Fitzmaurice & Catherine Flatley
m. July 1906 (John Ryan & Katie Sloyen), Bekan

Note: Martin was the son of John Fitzmaurice of Derrynacong. Catherine was the daughter of Andrew Flatley of Greenwood.

Katie Fitzmaurice & Henry Mannion
m. Nov. 1906 (Peter Hannin & Nora Fitzmaurice), Bekan

Note: Katie was the daughter of David Fitzmaurice of Togher. Henry was the son of Michael Mannion, dec'd., of Drumbaun.

Patrick Fitzmaurice & Mary Jordan
m. Apr. 1908 (Patrick Grealy & Mary Fitzmaurice), Annagh

Note: Patrick was the son of Michael Fitzmaurice of Forthill. Mary was the daughter of Patrick Jordan of Barheen.

Michael Fitzmaurice & Katie Travers
m. Apr. 1908 (Timothy Freeman & Maggie Carney), Bekan

Note: Michael was the son of John Fitzmaurice of Ballinacostello. Katie was the daughter of James Travers of Keebagh.

Ellen Fitzmaurice & Thomas Connolly
m. Apr. 1909 (Patrick Murphy & Kate Fitzmaurice), Annagh

Note: Ellen was the daughter of Michael Fitzmaurice of Spaddagh. Thomas was the son of Thomas Connolly of Carrickacat.

Bridget Fitzmaurice & James Sloyan
m. Apr. 1909 (Michael Sloyan & Norah Fitzmaurice), Bekan

Note: Bridget was the daughter of John Fitzmaurice of Brackloon North. James, a stone mason, was the son of Thomas Sloyan, dec'd., of Brackloon North.

John Fitzmaurice & Ellen Neary
m. Oct. 1910 (John Freyne & Maggie Dwyer), Bekan

Note: John, age 31, was the son of John Fitzmaurice, dec'd., of Culnacleha. Ellen, age 30, was the daughter of James Neary, dec'd., of Mountain.

David Fitzmaurice & Mary Beattie
m. Jan. 1911 (Martin Fitzmaurice & Bridget Beattie), Kiltullagh

Note: David, age 31 and a shopkeeper, was the son of David Fitzmaurice, dec'd., of Ballinlough. Mary, age 21, was the daughter of Edward Beattie of Ballinlough.

Timothy Fitzmaurice & Ellen Heneghan
m. Apr. 1912 (Francis Fitzmaurice & Mary Brennan)

Note: Timothy was the son of David Fitzmaurice of Togher. Ellen was the daughter of Thomas Heneghan of Cararea ?

James Fitzmaurice & Anne Hunt
m. Apr. 1913 (Thomas Fitzmaurice & Margaret Hunt), Bekan

Note: James, age 28, was the son of Michael Fitzmaurice of Spaddagh. Anne, age 27, was the daughter of John Hunt of Larganboy.

Patrick Fitzmaurice & Mary Horkan
m. June 1913 (Michael Fitzmaurice & Maggie Horkan), Bekan

Note: Patrick was the son of Martin Fitzmaurice of Treanrevagh. Mary was the daughter of James Horkan of Lassanny.

Patrick Fitzmaurice & Mary Commons
m. Dec. 1913 (Patrick McDonagh & Mary Commons), Loughglin

Note: Patrick was the son of Patrick Fitzmaurice of Brackloon. Mary was the daughter of John Commons of Clooncam.

Michael Fitzmaurice & Mary Culliney
m. Jan. 1914 (John Grealy & Maggie Flatley), Bekan

Note: Michael, a widower, was the son of Michael Fitzmaurice of Forthill. Mary was the daughter of Patrick Culliney of Tawnaghmore.

Mary Fitzmaurice & Patrick Carroll
m. Dec. 1914 (Timothy Flanagan & Maggie Fitzmaurice), Annagh

Mary, age 29, was the daughter of Mark Fitzmaurice of Barheen. Patrick, age 33, was the son of John Carroll of Derrylahan.

Mary Fitzmaurice & Michael Kelly
m. June 1915 (Thomas Kelly & Margaret Carney), Bekan

Note: Mary, age 35, was the daughter of Patrick Fitzmaurice of Reask. Michael, age 38, was the son of John Kelly of Lissaniska.

Mary Fitzmaurice & James Freyne
m. Feb. 1918 (John Freyne & Ana ? Fitzmaurice)

Note: Mary was the daughter of John Fitzmaurice of Ballyhaunis. James, a ship steward, was the son of Michael Freyne, Royal Barrack, Chatham.

Francis Fitzmaurice & Jane Lowry
m. Feb. 1918 (John Joseph Fitzmaurice & Katie Morris), Loughglin

Note: Francis was the son of John Fitzmaurice of Forthill. Jane was the daughter of Patrick Lowry of Erriff.

Catherine Fitzmaurice & Thomas McGarry
m. Apr. 1919 (Martin McGarry & Sarah Fitzmaurice), Bekan

Note: Catherine, age 29, was the daughter of John Fitzmaurice of Lisbaun. Thomas, age 28, was the son of Thomas McGarry of Cloontumper.

Timothy Fitzmaurice & Nora Kelly
m. Jan. 1920 (Edward Beattie & Mary O'Dowd), Bekan

Note: Timothy, a widower, was the son of David Fitzmaurice of Togher. Nora was the daughter of John Kelly of Brackloon.

Margaret Fitzmaurice & Thomas Kelly
m. Feb. 1921 (Michael Sloyan & Sarah Fitzmaurice), Bekan

Note: Margaret, age 27, was the daughter of John Fitzmaurice of Lisbaun. Thomas, age 33, was the son of John Kelly of Brackloon.

James Fitzmaurice & Margaret Carney
m. Feb. 1921 (Edward Carney & Norah Farrell), Bekan

Note: James, age 45, was the son of Patrick Fitzmaurice of Birkenhead, England. Margaret, age 25, was the daughter of Hugh Carney of Bekan.

Thomas Fitzmaurice & Sara Kavanagh
m. Apr. 1921 (John Fitzmaurice & Maggie McGrath), Claremorris

Note: Thomas was the son of Michael Fitzmaurice of Spaddagh. Sara was the daughter of John Kavanagh of Ballyglass.

Nora Fitzmaurice & John Higgins
m. Feb. 1922 (Michael Higgins & Mary Fitzmaurice), Bekan

Note: Nora was the daughter of Michael Fitzmaurice of Forthill. John was the son of John Higgins of Coolnafarna.

John Fitzmaurice & Norah Kelly
m. Augt. 1923 (James Kelly & Maggie Lydon), Kiltullagh

Note: John, age 40, was the son of Patrick Fitzmaurice of Tonregee. Norah, age 33, was the daughter of Thomas Kelly of Gorteen.

John Thomas Fitzmaurice & Bridget Agnes Hunt
m. March 1926 (Dominick Fitzmaurice & Margaret Hunt), Loughlin

Note: John Thomas was the son of Andrew Fitzmaurice & Bridget Flatley of Brackloon. Bridget Agnes was the daughter of Michael Hunt & Bridget Ganley of Tully.

Sarah Fitzmaurice & John Woods
m. June 1926 (Francis Ganley & Annie Dyer), Bekan

Note: Sarah was the daughter of John Fitzmaurice of Lisbaun. Thomas was the son of Thomas Woods of Cloonmaul ?

Ena Fitzmaurice & Patrick Harty
m. Feb. 1928 (John Harty & Gertrude Fitzmaurice), Ballyhaunis

Note: Ena was the daughter of John Charles Fitzmaurice of Ballyhaunis. Patrick, a civil servant, was the son of Michael Harty of Ballyhaunis.

Mary Fitzmaurice & Michael Sloyan
m. Apr. 1928 (John Connolly & N- Fitzmaurice), Bekan

Note: Mary was the daughter of Peter Fitzmaurice of Forthill. Michael was the son of James Sloyan of Brackloon.

Bridget Agnes Fitzmaurice & John Cosgrove
m. June 1930 (Paddy Cosgrove & Bridget Murphy), Bekan

Note: Bridget Agnes was the daughter of Andrew Fitzmaurice & Bridget Flatley of Brackloon. Bridget was the daughter of James Cosgrove of Erriff.

Michael Fitzmaurice & Eleanor Fitzmaurice
m. Nov. 1930 (Patrick Fitzmaurice & Mary K. Ganley), Bekan

Note: Michael was the son of John Fitzmaurice of Lisbaun. Eleanor was the daughter of John Fitzmaurice of Lisbaun.

Josephine Fitzmaurice & Peter Connolly
m. June 1931 (Patrick Fitzmaurice & Mary Hannon), Bekan

Note: Josephine, a dressmaker, was the daughter of Michael Connolly of Togher. Peter, a teacher, was the son of Peter Connolly of Bekan.

Catherine Fitzmaurice & Patrick McGuire
m. Sept. 1932 (William Jennings & Mary Fitzmaurice), Bekan

Note: Catherine was the daughter of Patrick Fitzmaurice of Forthill. Patrick was the son of Patrick McGuire of Mt. Delvin.

Delia Fitzmaurice & Francis Waldron
m. Feb. 1934 (John Fitzmaurice & Kathleen Doyle), Annagh

Note: Delia was the daughter of James Fitzmaurice of Derrylea. Francis was the son of Patrick Waldron of Ardarig ?

John Fitzmaurice & Cecilia Mullarkey
m. Apr. 1935 (Michael Fitzmaurice & Margaret Hussey), Annagh

Note: John was the son of Patrick Fitzmaurice of Abbeyquarter. Cecilia was the daughter of David Mullarkey of Tullaghaun.

Norah Fitzmaurice & Michael Keane
m. Apr. 1938 (John E. Gibbon & Kathleen Ferrie), Bekan

Note: Norah was the daughter of John Fitzmaurice of Forthill. Michael, a carpenter, was the son of Patrick Keane of Annagh, Aghamore.

Thomas Fitzmaurice & Catherine Plunkett
m. Apr. 1938 (Patrick Fitzmaurice & Eileen Comer ?), Annagh

Note: Thomas was the son of Thomas Fitzmaurice of Aglorah, Annagh. Catherine was the daughter of Thomas Plunkett of Curries, Annagh.

Bridget Fitzmaurice & Patrick Duffy
m. Feb. 1940 (Martin Duffy & Nellie Loftus), Annagh

Note: Bridget, age 32, was the daughter of Thomas Fitzmaurice of Lisduff. Patrick, age 35, was the son of Martin Duffy of (illegible).

Honoria Veronica Fitzmaurice & Patrick Taylor
m. Apr. 1940 (Francis Taylor & Sheila Fitzmaurice), Kiltullagh

Note: Honoria Veronica was the daughter of David Fitzmaurice of Ballinlough. Patrick was the son of Joseph Taylor of Kilkee ?

Fitzmaurice – Civil Death Records (informants in parentheses)

Thomas Fitzmaurice, Jan. 1870, 74, Pattenspark (Catherine Fitzmaurice, wife)
Patrick Fitzmaurice, Dec. 1870, 57, married, carpenter, Ballyhaunis (Coroner)
Honoria Fitzmaurice, March 1872, 9, Leo (Catherine Fitzmaurice)
Honoria Fitzmaurice, Apr. 1872, 70, married, Tonregee (Patrick Fitzmaurice)
Elizabeth Fitzmaurice, Apr. 1873, 48, widow of Patrick above (Denis Forde)
Michael Fitzmaurice, Apr. 1873, 34, married, Castle Quarter (Mary Fitzmaurice)
Patrick Fitzmaurice, Sept, 1873, 3 weeks, Forthill (Catherine Fitzmaurice)
Timothy Fitzmaurice, Feb. 1874, 3 weeks, Forthill (Ellen Fitzmaurice)
Ellen Fitzmaurice, June 1874, 55, widow, Cloonlee (Honor Gallagher)
Mark Fitzmaurice, July 1874, 70, married, Forthill (Ellen Fitzmaurice)
Julia Fitzmaurice, Jan. 1875, 17, Derrynacong (Mary Fitzmaurice)
David Fitzmaurice, Feb. 1875, 29, married, Mountain (Mary Fitzmaurice)
Patrick Fitzmaurice, Feb. 1875, 9, Coolatinny (Ellen Ryan)
Michael Fitzmaurice, June 1875, 17, Derrynacong (John Fitzmaurice)
Anne Fitzmaurice, June 1875, 3, Cherryfield (Debora Waldron)
Michael Fitzmaurice, Jan. 1876, 15 minutes, Lisbaun (Martin Flatley of Garraun)
Honoria Fitzmaurice, Jan. 1876, 83, widow, Togher (Timothy Fitzmaurice)
Bridget Fitzmaurice, Jan. 1876, 38, married, Bohaun (Patrick Fitzmaurice)

Child Fitzmaurice, Feb. 1876, 5 minutes, Lisbaun (John Fitzmaurice)

Anne Fitzmaurice, July 1876, 16, Reask (Peter Fitzmaurice of Larganboy)

Catherine Fitzmaurice, Augt. 1876, 37, married, Lisbaun (John Fitzmaurice)

Bridget Fitzmaurice, Sept. 1876, 40, Laughil, married (Mary Fitzmaurice)

Child Fitzmaurice, Sept. 1876, 2 days, Island (Patrick Fitzmaurice)

Sarah Fitzmaurice, Jan. 1877, 5, Mountain (John Grealy)

Kate Fitzmaurice, Augt. 1877, 3 weeks, Leo (Catherine Fitzmaurice)

Honoria Fitzmaurice, Sept. 1877, 7, Cherryfield (Bridget Fitzmaurice)

Mary Fitzmaurice, Feb. 1878, 78, Mountain (John Fitzmaurice)

Margaret Agnes Fitzmaurice, Apr. 1879, 4 days, Ballyhaunis (Sara McHugh)

Myles Fitzmaurice, June 1879, 60, married, Treanrevagh (Bridget Fitzmaurice)

Timothy Fitzmaurice, Augt. 1879, 1 day, Mountain (Francis Waldron)

Child Fitzmaurice, Feb. 1880, 10 minutes, Kilmannin (Patrick Fitzmaurice)

Mary Fitzmaurice, Apr. 1880, 21, Ballyhaunis (Denis Forde)

Margaret Fitzmaurice, Apr. 1880, 91 married, Treanrevagh (Martin Fitzmaurice)

Mary Fitzmaurice, Sept. 1880, 12, Shanvaghera (Mark Fitzmaurice)

David Fitzmaurice, Oct. 1880, 65, married, Brackloon (Catherine Henry)

Ellen Fitzmaurice, June 1882, 13, Tawnaghmore (Peter Fitzmaurice)

Patrick Fitzmaurice, Jan. 1883, 72, married, Barheen (Patrick Fitzmaurice, son)

Bridget Fitzmaurice, Feb. 1883, 3, Gorteen (Bridget Fitzmaurice, mother)

John Fitzmaurice, May 1883, 73, Brackloon (Margaret Fitzmaurice, wife)

Bridget Fitzmaurice, May 1883, 49, widow, Barheen (Patrick Fitzmaurice, son)

Mary Fitzmaurice, Sept. 1883, 62, married, Brackloon (Thomas Fitzmaurice, nephew)

Catherine Fitzmaurice, Apr. 1884, 80, widow, Forthill (Michael Fitzmaurice)

Margaret Fitzmaurice, Sept. 1884, 70, widow, Leo (Patrick Meehan of Leo)

James Fitzmaurice, Nov. 1885, 70, widower, Bekan (Martin Fitzmaurice, son)

Mary Fitzmaurice, June 1886, 56, married, Derrynacong (Mary Fitzmaurice, daughter)

Child Fitzmaurice, March 1887, 3 hours, Barheen (Mark Fitzmaurice, father)

Catherine Fitzmaurice, March 1887, 32, Barheen (Mark Fitzmaurice, husband)

Bridget Fitzmaurice, May 1887, 62, widow, Bekan (Mary Henry, daughter)

Margaret Fitzmaurice, Augt. 1887, 35, married, Lisbaun (Patrick McNamara)

Catherine Fitzmaurice, Oct. 1887, 71, widow, Lisbaun (Thomas Fitzmaurice, son-in-law)

John Fitzmaurice, Dec. 1887, 61, widower, Kilmannin (Catherine Fitzmaurice, daughter)

Sara Fitzmaurice, Feb. 1888, 4 months, Togher (Kate Fitzmaurice, sister)

Patrick Fitzmaurice, May 1888, 81, Togher (Patrick Gavin of Togher)

Mary Fitzmaurice, May 1888, 80, Woodpark (Patrick Fitzmaurice, husband)

Thomas Fitzmaurice, May 1889, 89, widower, Brackloon (Andrew Fitzmaurice, son)

Child Fitzmaurice, Nov. 1889, 3 hours, Barheen (Mary Fitzmaurice, grandmother)

Catherine Fitzmaurice, Nov. 1889, 3 days, Barheen (Mary Fitzmaurice, grandmother)

Bridget Fitzmaurice, Apr. 1890, 70, widow, Forthill (Honny Fitzmaurice)

Mary Fitzmaurice, March 1891, 84, widow, Gorteen (Michael Fitzmaurice, son)

John Fitzmaurice, Apr. 1891, 19, Leo (Catherine Fitzmaurice, mother)

Elizabeth Fitzmaurice, Apr. 1891, 55, Ballyhaunis (John C. Fitzmaurice, husband)

Honoria Fitzmaurice, June 1891, 4, Brackloon (Bridget Fitzmaurice, mother)

Thomas Fitzmaurice, Augt. 1891, 61, married, Lisduff (Thomas Byrne, son-in-law)

Child Fitzmaurice, Dec. 1891, 10 minutes, Barheen (Mark Fitzmaurice, father)

Child Fitzmaurice, March 1892, 10 minutes, Ballyhaunis (John C. Fitzmaurice, father)

Patrick Fitzmaurice, Jan. 1893, 66, widower, Woodpark (Mary Loftus, daughter)

Child Fitzmaurice, Apr. 1893, 10 minutes, Barheen (Mark Fitzmaurice, father)

John Fitzmaurice, Apr. 1893, 14 days, Derrylea (Catherine Fitzmaurice)

Bridget Fitzmaurice, July 1893, 80, widow, Brackloon (Mary Anne Sloyan, cousin)

Francis Fitzmaurice, Oct. 1893, 7 weeks, Ballyhaunis (John C. Fitzmaurice, father)

David Fitzmaurice, Nov. 1893, 80, Brackloon (Mary Fitzmaurice, wife)

Mary Josephine Fitzmaurice, Nov. 1893, 1, Cloonfad (Bridget Fitzmaurice)

Bridget Fitzmaurice, March 1894, 54, widow, Lisduff (Honor Fitzmaurice, daughter)

Peter Fitzmaurice, May 1895, 75, married, Larganboy (Mary Boyle)

Margaret Fitzmaurice, Augt. 1895, 75, widow, Brackloon (Margaret Fitzmaurice)

Catherine Fitzmaurice, Oct. 1895, 74, widow, Pattenspark (John Fitzmaurice, son)

Ellen Fitzmaurice, July 1896, 80, widow, Ballyhaunis (Edward Fitzmaurice, son)

Michael Fitzmaurice, Apr. 1896, 18, Leo (Catherine Fitzmaurice, mother)

Ellen Fitzmaurice, May 1896, 19, Cherryfield (Peter Fitzmaurice, father)

Martin Fitzmaurice, June 1896, 1, Gorteen (Bridget Fitzmaurice, mother)

Thomas Fitzmaurice, July 1896, 55, Forthill (Honny Fitzmaurice, wife)

Child Fitzmaurice, Sept. 1896, 5 minutes, Barheen (Mark Fitzmaurice, father)

Delia Fitzmaurice, Feb. 1897, 12, Ballyhaunis (Patrick Tarpey, stepfather)

Patrick Fitzmaurice, March 1897, 26, single, Leo (Catherine Fitzmaurice, mother)

Mary Fitzmaurice, May 1897, 78, widow, Brackloon (Bridget Tully, daughter)

James Fitzmaurice, Jan. 1899, 6 months, Brackloon (Andrew Fitzmaurice, father)

Thomas Fitzmaurice, Jan. 1899, 65, married, Leo (William Fitzmaurice, son)

John Fitzmaurice, Sept. 1899, 13, Ballyhaunis (Michael Fitzmaurice, brother)

Michael Fitzmaurice, Nov. 1899, 8 months, Forthill (Kate Fitzmaurice, mother)

Bridget Fitzmaurice, Jan. 1900, 60, Cherryfield (Peter Fitzmaurice, husband)

Anne Fitzmaurice, Feb.1901, 89, widow, Lisbaun (John Fitzmaurice, son)

Kate Fitzmaurice, Apr. 1901, 30, single, Gorteenbeg (Eleanor Fitzmaurice, mother)

Mark Fitzmaurice, May 1902, 25, single, Forthill (Michael Fitzmaurice, brother)

Thomas Fitzmaurice, July 1902, 77, Churchpark (Bridget Fitzmaurice, wife)

John Fitzmaurice, Apr. 1903, 58, single, Tonregee (Honny Fitzmaurice, sister-in-law)

Mary Fitzmaurice, Feb. 1904, 63, widow, Derrynacong (Catherine Waldron, daughter)

Patrick Fitzmaurice, June 1904, 2 days, Brackloon (Bridget Fitzmaurice)

Honoria Fitzmaurice, Oct. 1904, 70, married, Forthill (Michael Fitzmaurice)

James Fitzmaurice, Oct. 1904, 32, married, Tawnaghmore (Peter Fitzmaurice, father)

Patrick Mark Fitzmaurice, Oct. 1904, 5 months, Ballyhaunis (Bt. Waldron, Devlis, aunt)

Timothy Fitzmaurice, Nov. 1904, 63, married, Ballyhaunis (Claremorris workhouse)

David Fitzmaurice, Sept.1905, 66, Togher (Mary Fitzmaurice, wife)

John Fitzmaurice, July 1906, 68, married, Derrynacong (John Fitzmaurice, son)

Patrick Fitzmaurice, Nov. 1906, 83, widower, Derrynacong (Mary Regan, daughter)

Patrick Fitzmaurice, Apr. 1907, 71, widower, Lisbaun (Patrick Fitzmaurice, son)

Thomas Fitzmaurice, May 1907, 19, Forthill (Norah Fitzmaurice, mother)

Thomas Fitzmaurice, Feb. 1911, 35, married, Shanvaghera (Ellen Duffy, sister)

Catherine Fitzmaurice, March 1911, 75, married, Shanvaghera (Ellen Duffy, daughter)

Patrick Fitzmaurice, March 1911, 79, widower, Moigh, Castlerea (Mary Murray, niece)

Mary Fitzmaurice, Feb. 1912, 71, widow, Barheen, (Mark Fitzmaurice, son)

Bridget Fitzmaurice, May 1912, 24 days, Gorteenbeg (John Fitzmaurice, father)

Kate Fitzmaurice, Nov. 1912, 32, Forthill (Michael Fitzmaurice, husband)

Edward Fitzmaurice, Dec. 1912, 58, single, Ballyhaunis (Michael Lavan, cousin)

Catherine Fitzmaurice, Apr. 1913, 65, married, Clydagh (Margaret Fitzmaurice)

Timothy Fitzmaurice, July 1913, 67, widower, Shanvaghera (Timothy Fitzmaurice, son)

John Fitzmaurice, Sept. 1913, 60, married, Brackloon (Claremorris workhouse)

Edward Fitzmaurice, Dec. 1913, 3 years, Cherryfield (Mary Fitzmaurice, sister)

Norah Fitzmaurice, Jan. 1914, 49, Forthill (Peter Fitzmaurice, husband)

Ellen Fitzmaurice, March 1915, 42, Cherryfield (Peter Fitzmaurice, husband)

Michael Fitzmaurice, Augt. 1916, 72, married, Gorteen (Bridget Fitzmaurice, daughter)

Margaret Fitzmaurice, Sept. 1916, 8 months, Cherryfield (Claremorris workhouse)

Mary Fitzmaurice, Apr. 1917, 83, widow, Derrynacong (Mary Fitzmaurice, daughter)

John Fitzmaurice, Apr. 1917, 86, Pattenspark (Margaret Fitzmaurice, wife)

John C. Fitzmaurice, May 1917, 65, married, Ballyhaunis (James Waldron, b.in-law)

Patrick Fitzmaurice, Oct. 1917, 87, single, Treanrevagh (Catherine Fitzmaurice, s.-in-law)

Mary Fitzmaurice, Jan. 1918, 40, single, Derrynacong (Ellen Fitzmaurice, sister-in-law)

Stephen Fitzmaurice, Nov. 1918, 4, Cherryfield (William Fitzmaurice, brother)

Ellen Fitzmaurice, Nov. 1918, 33, Togher (Timothy Fitzmaurice, husband)

John Fitzmaurice, Dec. 1918, 85, widower, Clydagh (Maggie Fitzmaurice, d.-in-law)

Anne Fitzmaurice, March 1919, 74, married, Spaddagh (James Fitzmaurice, grandson)

Martin Fitzmaurice, March 1919, 6 weeks, Treanrevagh (Catherine Fitzmaurice, mother)

Thomas Fitzmaurice, Apr. 1919, 60, Cloonfad (Bridget Fitzmaurice, wife)

Mary Fitzmaurice, July 1919, 77, widow, Togher (Timothy Fitzmaurice, son)

Mary Fitzmaurice, Nov. 1920, 65, married, Ballyhaunis (Margaret Fitzmaurice, daughter)

Patrick Fitzmaurice, Feb. 1921, 80, Reask (Mary Fitzmaurice, wife)

John Fitzmaurice, Nov. 1922, 84, widower, Lisbaun (Sarah Fitzmaurice, daughter)

Peter Fitzmaurice, Jan. 1923, 86, married, Ballyhaunis (Bridget Murry, niece, Derrintogh.)

John Fitzmaurice, July 1923, 86, married, Mountain (Francis Fitzmaurice, son)

Peter Fitzmaurice, Feb. 1924, 1, Castleplunkett (D. Fitzmaurice)

Patrick Fitzmaurice, Feb. 1924, 1, Castleplunkett (D. Fitzmaurice, father)

David Fitzmaurice, March 1924, 58, Tullaghaun (Bridget Fitzmaurice, wife)

Bridget Fitzmaurice, July 1924, 4 days, Ballinlough (David Fitzmaurice, father)

Michael Fitzmaurice, Nov. 1924, 92, widower, Spaddagh (James Fitzmaurice, son)

Michael Fitzmaurice, Jan. 1925, 76, married, Togher (Michael Fitzmaurice, son)

Patrick Fitzmaurice, Apr. 1925, 86, widower, Barheen (A. Jordan, cousin)

Martin Fitzmaurice, May 1925, 86, married, Treanrevagh (Mary Fitzmaurice, daughter)

John Fitzmaurice, Nov. 1926, 70, Forthill (Catherine Fitzmaurice, wife)

Bridget Fitzmaurice, Jan. 1927, 15, Tonregee (Norah Fitzmaurice, sister)

James Fitzmaurice, March 1927, 83, Derrylea (Kathleen Fitzmaurice, wife)

Catherine Fitzmaurice, June 1928, 81, widow, Treanrevagh (Mary Fitzmaurice, sister)

Patrick Fitzmaurice, July 1928, 64, Tawnaghmore (Mary Fitzmaurice, wife)

Patrick Fitzmaurice, Oct. 1928, 81, widower, Ballyhaunis (Coroner)

Jane Fitzmaurice, Apr. 1929, 38, Mountain (Francis Fitzmaurice, husband)

Andrew Fitzmaurice, Apr. 1929, 85, Brackloon North (Bridget Fitzmaurice, wife)

Kate Fitzmaurice, July 1929, 29, married, Castleplunkett (D. Fitzmaurice)

Bridget Fitzmaurice, March 1930, 77, widow, Gorteen (Bridget Judge, daughter)

Louis Sylvester Fitzmaurice, June 1930, 1, Cloonfad (Luke Fitzmaurice, father)

Bridget Fitzmaurice, June 1931, 75, widow, teacher, Cloonfad (Luke Fitzmaurice)

Honoria Fitzmaurice, May 1931, 85, widow, Forthill (Patrick Fitzmaurice)

Martin Fitzmaurice, Sept. 1932, 52, single, Reask (Katie Fitzmaurice, sister)

John Joseph Fitzmaurice, Nov. 1932, 35, single, Cloonfad (? Fitzmaurice, brother)

Mark Fitzmaurice, Apr. 1933, 79, married, Barheen (Delia Fitzmaurice, daughter)

Andrew Fitzmaurice, July 1933, 52, married, Cloonfad (Coroner)

Bridget Fitzmaurice, July 1933, 78, widow, Barheen (Delia Fitzmaurice, daughter)

Patrick Fitzmaurice, Dec. 1933, 73, widower, Abbeyquarter (Cath. McGuire, daughter)

Peter Fitzmaurice, March 1934, 75, widower, Forthill (Nora Fitzmaurice, daughter)

Thomas Fitzmaurice, Apr. 1934, 73, married, Lisduff (Bridget Fitzmaurice, daughter)

Michael Fitzmaurice, June 1934, 26, single, Clydagh (Austin Fitzmaurice)

Mary Fitzmaurice, Sept. 1936, 69, widow, Tawnaghmore (Thomas Fitzmaurice, son)

Michael Emmett Fitzmaurice, Jan. 1937, 25, single, Forthill (John J. Fitzmaurice, brother)

Patrick Fitzmaurice, Oct. 1937, 84, widower, Derrylea (Delia Waldron, daughter)

Mary Fitzmaurice, Feb. 1939, 78, single, Leo (John Joe Fitzmaurice, nephew)

Katherine Fitzmaurice, Dec. 1939, 77, widow, Lisduff (Bridget Fitzmaurice, daughter)

Patrick Fitzmaurice, Apr. 1940, 76, Barheen (Mary Fitzmaurice, wife)

Gretta Fitzmaurice, May 1940, 16, Greenwood (Imelda Fitzmaurice, sister)

1901 Census – Annagh Civil Parish – Heads of Household Alphabetized by Townland

Aderg	– Bridget Fitzmaurice, 60, widow
Arglora	– Thomas Fitzmaurice, 40, & Catherine Fitzmaurice, 36
Ballyhaunis	– John C. Fitzmaurice, 50, & Mary Fitzmaurice, 28
Barheen	– Mark Fitzmaurice, 40, & Bridget Fitzmaurice, 39
	Mary Fitzmaurice, 70, widow
Barheen	– Patrick Fitzmaurice, 55 & Bridget Fitzmaurice, 54
Derrylea	– James Fitzmaurice, 50, & Catherine Fitzmaurice, 47
Derrynacong	– John Fitzmaurice, 80, & Mary Fitzmaurice, 67
Derrynacong	– Michael Regan, 40, & Mary Regan, 37
	Patrick Fitzmaurice, 76, widower
Gorteen	– Michael Fitzmaurice, 50, & Bridget Fitzmaurice, 45
Grallagh	– Thomas Fitzmaurice, 70, & Bridget Fitzmaurice, 52
Leo	– Catherine Fitzmaurice, 50, widow
Pattenspark	– John Fitzmaurice, 60, & Maggie Fitzmaurice, 40
Spaddagh	– Michael Fitzmaurice, 56, & Anne Fitzmaurice, 50
Tonregee	– Patrick Fitzmaurice, 65, & Anne Fitzmaurice, 52

1901 Census – Bekan Civil Parish – Heads of Household Alphabetized by Townland

Ballyhaunis	– Patrick Fitzmaurice, 45, & Mary Fitzmaurice, 40

Ballyhaunis	~ Patrick Tarpey, 39, & Mary Tarpey, 39
	Mary Ellen Fitzmaurice, 20, & Maggie
	Fitzmaurice, 17, stepdaughters
Ballyhaunis	~ Katie Fitzmaurice, 23, & Maggie
	Conway, 15, apprentice
Ballyhaunis	~ William Murphy, 53, & Margaret Murphy, 40
	Honor Fitzmaurice, 56, mother-in-law
Ballyhaunis	~ Edward Fitzmaurice, 38, & Ellen
	Fitzmaurice, 25, sister
Ballyhaunis	~ Peter Fitzmaurice, 60 & Margaret McGarry, 50
Brackloon North	~ Andrew Fitzmaurice, 40, & Bridget Fitzmaurice, 38
Brackloon North	~ John Fitzmaurice, 50, & Catherine Fitzmaurice, 40
Bekan	~ Martin Fitzmaurice, 62, & Catherine Fitzmaurice, 50
Cherryfield	~ Peter Fitzmaurice, 33, & Ellen Fitzmaurice, 29
	Peter Fitzmaurice, 65, widower
Forthill	~ Honoria Fitzmaurice, 52, widow
Forthill	~ Michael Fitzmaurice, 74, & Sarah Fitzmaurice, 68
Forthill	~ Michael Fitzmaurice, 60, & Norah Fitzmaurice, 55
Gorteenbeg	~ Patrick Fitzmaurice, 75, & Ellen Fitzmaurice, 60
Kilmannin	~ Patrick Fitzmaurice, 40, & Kate Fitzmaurice, 38
Lisbaun East	~ John Fitzmaurice, 60, & Mary Fitzmaurice, 43
Lisbaun East	~ Patrick Fitzmaurice, 65, widower
Mountain	~ John Fitzmaurice, 60, & Bridget Fitzmaurice, 50
Reask	~ Patrick Fitzmaurice, 60, & Mary Fitzmaurice, 49
Reask	~ Patrick Byrne, 50, & Mary Byrne, 49
	Patrick J. Fitzmaurice, 82, & Bridget Fitzmaurice, 72
Tawnaghmore	~ James Fitzmaurice, 28, & Norah Fitzmaurice, 29
	Celia Flatley, 60, aunt, widow
Tawnaghmore	~ Patrick Fitzmaurice, 40, & Mary Fitzmaurice, 35
	Bridget Fitzmaurice, 70, widow
Togher	~ David Fitzmaurice, 60, & Mary Fitzmaurice, 50
Togher	~ Michael Fitzmaurice, 41, single

1901 Census ~ Kiltullagh Civil Parish ~ Heads of Household Alphabetized by Townland

Ballinlough   ~ David Fitzmaurice, 21, in home of Michael Keane, 31, & Kate Keane, 27

[David was the son of David Fitzmaurice & Mary Hannon of Togher]

Cloonfad West ~ Thomas Fitzmaurice, 41, & Bridget Fitzmaurice, 46

Clydagh Upper ~ John Fitzmaurice, 65, & Catherine Fitzmaurice, 60

Laughil   ~ Patrick Fitzmaurice, 70, widower

Calendar of Wills

Thomas Fitzmaurice of Pattenspark
died 17 Jan. 1870
beneficiary – Catherine Fitzmaurice, wife
effects – under 100 pounds

Patrick Fitzmaurice of Ballyhaunis
died 18 Dec. 1870
beneficiary – Elizabeth Fitzmaurice, wife
effects – under 200 pounds

Michael Fitzmaurice of Castlequarter
died 9 May 1888 [Note: no civil record has been located]
beneficiary – Thomas Fitzmaurice, brother
effects – 157 pounds

Thomas Fitzmaurice of Leo
died 7 Apr. 1899
beneficiary – Catherine Fitzmaurice, wife
effects – 51 pounds

Mary Fitzmaurice of Derrynacong
died 4 Feb. 1904

beneficiary – Catherine Waldron, wife of James Waldron
effects – 9 pounds, 16 shillings

James Fitzmaurice of Tawnaghmore
died 4 Oct. 1904
beneficiary – Honoria Fitzmaurice, wife
effects – 54 pounds

David Fitzmaurice of Togher
died 21 Sept. 1905
beneficiary – Mary Fitzmaurice, wife
effects – 71 pounds

Patrick Fitzmaurice of Derrynacong
died 6 Nov. 1906
beneficiary – Mary Regan, wife of Michael Regan
effects – 86 pounds

Timothy Fitzmaurice of Shanvaghera, Knock
died 21 July 1913
beneficiary – Timothy Fitzmaurice
effects – 101 pounds, 18 shillings

Ellen Fitzmaurice of Ballyhaunis, spinster
died 25 March 1915
beneficiary – Michael Fitzmaurice
effects – 104 pounds, 1 shilling

John Fitzmaurice of Pattenspark
died 30 Apr. 1917
beneficiary – Margaret Fitzmaurice, wife
effects – 189 pounds, 10 shillings

John C. Fitzmaurice of Ballyhaunis
died 10 May 1917
beneficiary – Mary Fitzmaurice, wife
effects – 815 pounds